1983

FANTASY LITERATURE

By the same author

Novels

SILKEN LINES AND SILVER HOOKS

ADONIS' GARDEN

Criticism

THOMAS MANN: The Devil's Advocate

VIRGINIA WOOLF: A Study of her Novels

FANTASY LITERATURE

An Approach to Reality

T.E. APTER

Indiana University Press
Bloomington

Library of Congress Cataloging in Publication Data

Apter, T. E.
  Fantasy literature.

  Includes index.
  1. Fantastic fiction — History and criticism.
  2. Psychoanalysis and literature. I. Title.
  PN3435.A65   809.3′ 876   82–47794
  ISBN 0–253–32101–8   AACR2
  1 2 3 4 5 86 85 84 83 82

To my father

Contents

Acknowledgements

The author and publishers wish to thank the following who have kindly given permission for the use of copyright material:

Sigmund Freud Copyrights Ltd, the Institute of Psycho-Analysis, and the Hogarth Press Ltd, for permission to quote from *The Standard Edition of the Complete Psychological Works of Sigmund Freud,* translated and edited by James Strachey.

Martin Secker & Warburg Ltd for permission to quote from *In the Penal Settlement* by Franz Kafka, translated by Willa and Edwin Muir.

Schocken Books Inc for permission to reprint from *The Penal Colony* by Franz Kafka, copyright © 1948 by Schocken Books Inc. Copyright renewed © 1965 by Schocken Books Inc.

Penguin Books Ltd for permission to quote from Nikolai Gogol's *Diary of a Madman and Other Stories* by Nikolai Gogol, translated by Ronald Wilks.

Calder and Boyars Ltd for permission to quote from E.T.A. Hoffmann's *The Devil's Elixirs,* translated by Ronald Taylor.

The author gives special thanks to Dr Nathaniel S. Apter for his comments, criticism and encouragement.

1 Introduction: Fantasy and Psychoanalysis

The aim and purpose of fantasy in literature are not necessarily different from those of the most exacting realism. What is called 'truth' in fiction is often hypothetical: if a character has certain traits, then one is likely to find, or enlightened by finding in him, other, related traits; also, if a character has certain traits then his actions and responses are already to some extent circumscribed. Yet hypotheses in fiction, however 'realistic', must be imaginative as well as plausible. At each state in the work the artist is faced with choices and decisions that may not have been foreseen at a previous stage. The 'truth' of fiction is attributable not only to the integration of character traits, the balance of motives, the consequences of actions and the development of events, but also to the ways in which new plausibilities are spotted, and the ways in which the artist's decisions create possibilities which throw light on various characters, their motives, or their conditions. Truth in fiction is not a study of probabilities but a utilisation and discovery of both possibilities and plausibilities to make points about what is probably our world.

As practised readers of fiction we can gauge the point and legitimacy of conclusions drawn from fantastic as well as from realistic premises. For example, when Gregor Samsa wakes to find himself transformed into a gigantic insect, then his and his family's subsequent behaviour reveals a great deal about Gregor's pre-insectile state and thus justifies Kafka's use of the implausible premise. The fantastic circumstances can be viewed as an economical and effective means of revealing characters' interests and emotions which would be disguised or modified in surroundings well ordered by comfort or custom; in this way they would be seen to have the same purpose as the realist's plot.

Alternatively, though not exclusively, the fantastic tale may be read as an allegory, with the literal story seen as a hieroglyph recording a previously established truth. The fantastic occurrences, setting, or characters will not tax the reader's credulity for they will be treated as systematic representations, with the particular quality of their strangeness commenting in various ways upon the ideas represented.

These suggestive readings make fantasy respectable and manageable, but they are obviously inadequate. If fantasy is a story proceeding logically from a fantastic premise, then the bizarre expectations it arouses and its peculiar brand of reasoned confusion are ignored. If the mental acrobatics of the fantasist are treated as allegories, then their revolutionary constructions are ignored. In either case fantasy becomes inessential to the work's themes and ideas, however appropriate it may be to their presentation. My aim in this book is to discuss the methods and achievements of fantasy in the modern novel and story, from Nathaniel Hawthorne to Jorge Luis Borges, and to show how and why fantasy is essential to the authors' various purposes, which must be understood not as an escape from reality but as an investigation of it. The works discussed here are different from the fairy tale, myth or saga which are either enacted in a world separated from ours spatially or temporally (in a 'Never-never land' or 'Once upon a time'), or which are imaginative, emblematic histories. The respective metamorphoses of Jove and the Beast are very different from Gregor Samsa's because, however wonderful, they occur within the laws of their mythic or enchanted settings. Gregor Samsa's transformation obviously breaks natural laws: if the tale is not understood as occuring within our world it loses its point. However, at the same time that Gregor's transformation defies nature and logic, it reveals an unexpected order which indubitably belongs to our world. Recognition is puzzling not only because it is disturbing but also because of the strangely literal language fantasy employs and the difficulty in marking out that area of thought, response and perception which is thereby realistically decribed.

At the heart of fantasy in modern fiction is the uncertainty as to which world the tale belongs—to this one, or to a very different one? The central query is unlike Hamlet's uncertainty as to the status of the ghost — an illusion, a demon, an angel, his dead father? — and unlike, too, the query in *The Turn of the Screw* — are the ghosts hallucinated or are they spectres which could, in principle, be seen by others? The problematic fantasies in Hawthorne, Conrad, Hoffmann, Kafka, Gogol, Dostoevsky, Nabokov and Borges cannot be isolated within a generally stable world, nor can answers as to the status of the fantasies solve the questions they raise. Even if Gogol's madman or Dostoevsky's Golyadkin or Hoffmann's Nathanael have got things wrong, their beliefs, expectations and perceptions persist in commenting upon this world. The impact of fantasy rests upon the fact that the world presented seems to be unquestionably ours, yet at the same time, as in a dream, ordinary meanings are suspended. Everything proliferates with potential meanings and becomes a potential danger. Even when a mistake is seen to be made, the fear is not mitigated. The ideas, objects and situations remain hedged round with baffling associations. All reassurance or reprieve is illusory in face of the anxiety arising from the knowledge that the familiar can take on, and tends to take on, strange and threatening forms.

The discontinuity of image and pattern essential to fantasy defies the systematic representations of allegory. More strongly, the fantasist's terms should not be read wholly metaphorically, however allusive they may be, for the function of metaphor is to persuade the audience that one thing can be seen as another, thereby revealing new aspects of either term. The poet, or any master-metaphorist, invites us to change, even to take risks with our perceptions, but the fantasist has already passed beyond warning signs into the danger area. However figurative his language, there is no 'vehicle' or 'tenor', no means of finding the way back to original terms. Metaphor makes it possible to employ extreme and original language without being lost among strange representations. One term can be considered in the light of another without losing its identity. Or, if a term does come, by way of metaphor, either to lose its original meaning or to have its meaning extended, the initial metaphoric thrust is subdued by common usage and the new use of the term becomes another example of the strongly metaphoric tendency of language itself; it now registers rather than challenges prevailing presuppositions and associations. The fantasist's metaphors, however, combine the conflation of vehicle and tenor with strange and new associations; figurative language becomes the only means of making literal assertions, for ordinary meanings fragment, expand, splinter, either because some new, unknown order prevails, or because the former order functions haphazardly or piecemeal. Thus the fantasist must piece together a new language.

Coleridge's well-known distinction between Fancy and Imagination, in which the former capacity creates an artefact whose elements are, though assembled, distinct and unintegrated, whereas the later creates a product whose elements are mutually dependent and richly, perhaps interminably allusive, bears no reference to the qualities of fantasy, for though 'fantasy' is sometimes shortened to 'fancy' the two terms generally have a different use. Nonetheless fantasy is frequently contrasted with imagination in ways which parallel Coleridge's distinction. Fantasy is unconscious, uncontrolled, highly personal, and its products lack integration or generality or balance. Here fantasy is linked to the day dream, to easy solutions, to egoism and escapism, in contrast with the reality-testing imagination. Nor do all slights upon fantasy bear this post-Freudian stamp. Fantasy is frequently linked to mistaken or misguided beliefs and perceptions, or to specifically unrealistic characteristics. Mercutio describes his vision of Queen Mab as dreams

> Which are the children of an idle brain,
> Begot of nothing but vain fantasy;
> Which is as thin of substance as the air,
> And more inconstant than the wind,[1]

though Shakespeare's use of Mercutio's speech to register the grotesque forces within Romeo's ecstasy challenges the character's dismissal.

In the sense in which fantasy is contrasted with imagination, it may lead to non-fantastic as easily as to fantastic creations. Though it is postulated as a mental activity its mark in artistic products is artistic poverty of a special kind. The work crippled by fantasy in this sense attempts crude satisfactions of personal desires, seeking simple solutions rather than resolutions to problems; or it may reveal idiosyncratic and unpersuasive associations, or tediously harp upon personal anger, or fail to communicate its meaning. This use of 'fantasy' is obviously different from the characterisation of fantasy literature, though there are similarities which justify the use of the same term.

Fantasy literature employs associations which are like idiosyncratic associations. Initially their strangeness may appear to be incoherent, and thus either dead to allusion or triggering off wayward, inconclusive strings of allusion. The fragmented perception, the mingling of trivial and gargantuan meanings, the anxious and inept quest for certainty, bear the mark of egoism, not only because their emphasis is on personal fear but also because the difficulties seem to arise from some flaw within the ego. There is often the impression, too, as in the case of literature impeded by fantasy, that fantasy in literature emerges from unconscious beliefs and has as its aim the satisfaction of unconscious desires. Moreover, in its display of dream characteristics, fantasy literature is peculiarly susceptible to psychoanalytic interpretations of dreams. In bearing the mark of unconscious processes—timelessness, fragmentation, mutual contradiction, exaggeration, distortion, displacement, condensation — it tempts the critic to read such literature as an exhibition of unconscious processes. The structure of fantasy literature often leaves the impression that the work has not been executed under conscious control, for many fine fantasy tales are not 'well wrought urns' but ungainly forms, with proliferations and fragmentations of theme and cruelly unresolved conclusions. Frequently the vitality of the fantasist's representations arises from abrasiveness and imbalance; the impact of fantasy seems to depend upon unresolved and disguised emotions.

Psychoanalytic theory, so adept at defying absurdity, is a plausible aid to interpretation of this difficult and dubious genre. Yet the special fascination psychoanalysis holds here must be 'placed' in the context of a criticism of fantasy literature which distinguishes between impediment by fantasy and the achievements of fantasy. The unconscious material utilised in fantasy literature is that which is ordinarily controlled by ordinary language and presuppositions essential to normal functioning. Fantasy is the means by which such material is exposed and investigated. Only in creating new associations and expectations can language set to work in this area. The characteristics fantasy shares with unconscious processes do not necessarily indicate artistic impediment.

In the *Convivio* Dante defined *Fantasia* as the representation of the intellect's dream, and though his use of fantasy as 'visionary imagination' is now archaic, a link between fantasy and dream seems inescapable. Yet for Dante the dream had a respectability which the modern dream lacks. Dante's dream belonged to the intellect. Its revelatory power stemmed from the fact that it was controlled, systematic, abstract. The modern conception of dream can be viewed as a development of the Romantic dream which is product of faculties in opposition to the intellect. The Romantics's dream, too, provided enlightenment, but in a somewhat disreputable and rebellious fashion in contrast to the prevailing esteem for reason. The Romantics sought the strange and exciting within themselves and were stimulated by the assumption that dream would disclose baffling and powerful inner forces. Psychoanalysis, in regard to its emphasis on beliefs and desires inadmissable to consciousness, and on the role of the irrational in the determination of human behaviour, can be viewed as an outgrowth of the Romantic glorification of emotion and impulse, for Romantic artists valued irrational influences, however controlled their imaginations in fact were.

The psychoanalytic treatment of the dream differs in an important respect from that of the Romantics, for the means by which psychoanalysis endorses the unconscious and its fantasies are also the means by which it derides them. In insisting that dreams and products of the imagination, especially those products characterised as fantastic, have significance, that even the most bizarre and apparently nonsensical mental creations have meaning, psychoanalytic theory endorses these products;

but in explicating their meaning in terms of unconscious sexual fantasies attributable variously to the artist, his characters or his audience, their point and purpose is trivialised. The fantasist's use of distortion, his defiance of logic and of time, his sensitivity to ill-defined and highly personal forces, his use of fragmenting and fusing personalities is granted meaning but deprived of its artistic purpose. Psychoanalytic interpretation tends to constrict language within the sphere of unconscious personal or human history, forcing its references back to repressed desires and discarded beliefs despite its desperate attempts to delineate human reality.

Responses to psychoanalytic interpretation are ambivalent. Fantasy now is not only respectable but fashionable. Any fantasy, from folk and fairy tales to science fiction and children's tales, is valued as an introduction to unconscious material. The 'depth' of the unconscious as a metaphoric placing in the psychic structure is associated with depth in the sense of profundity. Any image or tale amenable to psychoanalytic interpretation is treated as meaningful in the strong, poetic sense. With Jung's help, the possibility that fantastic ideas are as susceptible to platitude as intellectual ones is usually ignored.

However, common sense and a little experience tell us that fantasy literature varies enormously not only in quality but in purpose. In both old and modern fairy stories fantasy provides the thread of reason which can restore peace and harmony. Fantasy offers escape from reality, but the purpose and effect of the escape ranges from wish-fulfilment, excitement or sheer entertainment, to release from habitual assumptions, thus providing a vantage point from which new possibilities can be realised. In most fairy tales fantasy implements hope, opening up the possibility of resolving even the most recalcitrant defeats and fears. Tolkien, in his essay 'On Fairy Stories', describes the fairy tale as a means of setting free needs and desires, confirming the validity of their pursuit and fulfilment, presenting the recovery of fragmented or lost desires, and thus also offering consolation. In the modern novels and stories discussed in this book fantasy also serves as a means of escaping from habitual assumptions and expectations, but the purpose of this escape is to show how awful, how limiting and imprisoning, the human world is. Fantasy discovers and aggravates disintegraton. It is not a means of consolation and recovery but of registering losses and fears. Thus such fantasy is predominately 'negative' in that it does not resolve problems but rather magnifies them. To expect a more 'positive' or optimistic message would be to ignore the very issues which fantasy differentiates from the ordinarily bland mass of perceptions, desires and expectations.

Fantasy provides a point of vantage from which we are shown the gaps in our knowledge. Such gaps impede self-realisation because they make predictions, and the decisions which are based upon predictions, impossible. Unable to act responsibly, we feel subject to a variety of forces. The impediments to self-realisation become humiliations. The self feels responsible for its ignorance and confusion, indeed for its very irresponsibility. Ignorance and confusion may be universal, but it seems that only select characters are sensitive to them. The truly ignorant and insensitive are the proud and cruel surviviors, whereas the one who is especially aware is crippled by the truths he perceives. Even in cases in which impediments to self-realisation are external, they tend to have highly individual effects as though they were internal impediments. Thus are they closely related to the psychic disturbances whose motives and mechanisms it was Freud's purpose to expose.

It is beginning to be acknowledged, however, by critics as well as analysts, that literature cannot simply be submitted to the prestige and authority of psychoanalysis.[2] Previously literature was considered more or less as something to be interpreted, whereas psychoanalysis was knowledge, the master-interpreter of fictions and visions. Psychoanalysis found its predecessors in literature, and named many of its themes after literary figures (Oedipus, Narcissus); but, it was supposed, literary precursors had not systematised the themes now appropriated by psychoanalysis. Yet the systematisation of psychoanalysis not only shares obvious features with fiction in general but in particular with the logic and rhetoric of fantasy. This is not to deny psychoanalysis its own clinical sphere, but rather to suggest that its theories and interpretations should be more pliant towards literary influences, and that, with special regard to its theories of fantasy, it must look at what fantasy in the modern novel and story reveals about psychoanalytic theories and procedures, and, accordingly, modify its central notions as to the possible functions and aims of fantasy. In this book I suggest that fantasy can explore and test reality in much the same manner as psychoanalysis, and, moreover, that the least misleading approach to psychoanalysis is as to an example of fantasy literature, without ignoring the fascinating implications of psychoanalysis to individual works of fantasy. Freud's works, in particular, then become a magically rich text, rather than a body of theoretical knowledge.

However, any purely literary challenge to psychoanalytic theory must proceed with caution, well aware of its limitations. Psychoanalytic theory attempts to explain human behaviour, in particular the role of unconscious beliefs and desires in behaviour; its aim is not to explain human artefacts. Fantasy in literature, however 'neurotic' its content, has undergone (usually a good deal of) conscious modification; primary fantasy, which is the psychoanalyst's quarry, has been worked over by the secondary processes (i.e. thought), thereby endowing the primitive fantasy with reality-tested derivations.

Nonetheless, Freud himself vacillates from marking out the boundaries between psychoanalysis and art, to using the former as master over the latter. In 'Dostoevsky and Parricide' (1928) he claims that 'before the problem of the creative artist analysis must, alas, lay down its arms,' and in his essay on Leonardo (1910) he writes that though artistic productivity is intimately connected with sublimation (that is, the transformation of sexual or destructive impulses into socially acceptable activity), the nature of artistic attainment is inaccessible to psychoanalysis. In *Beyond the Pleasure Principle* (1920) he acknowledges that psychoanalysis searches for the operation of exceedingly primitive tendencies; phenomena as sophisticated as art works and artistic creativeness are not its concern.[3] More often than not, however, he proceeds to discuss art in complete ignorance of his modest disclaimers. In 'Creative Writers and Day-Dreaming' (1908) and 'Psychopathic Characters on the Stage' (1915) the only aspect of creativity that puzzles Freud is the artist's capacity to make the expression of his egoistic and neurotic fantasies palatable to others and to distract the audience sufficiently to encourage enjoyment of ordinarily inadmissible desires.

How is it that psychoanalytic theory is so easily tempted into the artistic sphere? It is based upon psychoanalytic technique which employs free association, attention to resistance (i.e., to obstacles to free association), interpretation of dreams and interpretation of transferences. These techniques involve the subject's participation, which the psychoanalytic critic does not have. The material in art, too, is different from that upon with psychoanalytic theory is based. In the analytic session the material uncovered is subject to change in response to the analyst's interventions — interpretations, questions, efforts at clarification, affective displays — and even to adventitious events within the consulting room. The temptation to apply psychoanalytic theory to art works arises, first, from Freud's and his followers' repeated references to art works which often did uncover new material; and, secondly, it arises from aspects of Freud's theories which grant plausibility to the application of psychoanalysis outside the consulting room and independent of psychoanalytic techniques. For Freud's initial emphasis on unconscious factors in the determination of human behaviour revealed time as bound: present behaviour and associations indicated past desires, renunciations, displaced meanings, fantasies and beliefs. Thus a history could be read off from present material. In addition, certain associations and patterns, in particular the Oedipal phase and its concomitant complexes (e.g., the castration complex) and developments (e.g., the super-ego), were seen as both central and universal. Sufficient confirmation was thought to be found in clinical work to apply it to cases that could not be clinically investigated. Literary works in particular were seen to deal with desires, fears, unknown and unacknowledged motives, influences and aims, thus offering an opportunity for analysis. Moreover, artistic works were themselves the products of imagination, which has obvious links with primitive fantasy, and therefore the author's unconscious desires and aims might be gleaned from his work on similar if not identical principles to those upon which primitive fantasy is attributed in the analytic session.

Such applications of psychoanalytic theory challenge the heuristic account of the truth of psychoanalytic interpretation put forward in defence of the charge that analytic statements are unverifiable. That interpretation is 'true' which, when accepted by the patient, leads to the amelioration of symptoms. This account of truth rests upon the theory that the bringing forward of unconscious material to consciousness is therapeutic; the experiences or fantasies upon which psychic disturbances depend are repeated in analysis, and the repetition reduces the accompanying excitation to a manageable level. It may be that repetition does not require a highly accurate description of the original material. A rough sketch, or even an analogous version, may be sufficiently suggestive. Even so, psychoanalytic interpretation is not tantamount to a drug whose adequacy is gauged only in terms of its effectiveness. Though interpretations need to be adequate rather than accurate, their adequacy depends upon their ability to aim at the truth. The effectiveness of psychoanalytic interpretation is a consequence, not the content of its truth. Therefore attributions of accuracy and validity, or the reverse, to psychoanalytic interpretations of art works, which cannot be tested by their effects upon symptoms, can be squared with psychoanalytic theory.

The mutual attraction of psychoanalysis and literary criticism is also based upon the similarity psychoanalysis has to art, a similarity which, I suggest, is far from superficial. The irreducibly figurative character of many central psychoanalytic terms — 'drive', 'libido', 'boundary', 'defence' — has recently been pointed out by several critics,[4] as, previously, Freud's descriptions of unconscious processes in the dream work had been seen as apt descriptions of literary techniques.[5] But of course Freud himself was the first and most meticulous recorder of the literary tendencies of his work. In *Studies on Hysteria* (1895) he says, 'it strikes me myself as strange that the case histories I write should read like short stories and that, as one might say, they lack the serious stamp of science. I must console myself with the reflection that the nature of the subject is evidently responsible for this, rather than any preference of my own.'[6] In *The Interpretation of Dreams* (1900-01) Freud defends his metaphorical treatment of ideas as images with the argument that accessory representations may be kept extrinsic from that which they 'dissect', though he admits that in the process of representing the mental apparatus within the mental apparatus, the layers of language are difficult to keep apart; and, indeed, in *Beyond the Pleasure Principle* (1920) he not only acknowledges the irreducibly speculative nature of psychoanalysis but also exhibits its centrally figurative language, 'picturing' as he does the psyche as a 'living vesicle' with a 'receptive cortical layer', the outermost surface of which consists of a 'membrane' which has been 'baked through' so that it becomes a 'protective shield against stimuli', necessary because the psyche is 'a little fragment of living substance . . . suspended in the middle of an external world charged with the most powerful energies.'[7] In *New Introductory Lectures* (1933) he admits that the layers of meaning he once thought distinguishable cannot be kept apart and that the id must be approached with analogies.[8]

The persistence with which psychoanalysis turns itself into literature is grounded in two problems. First, the nature of the enterprise — that of employing the mind to discover its own processes and mechanisms which are often deliberately elusive, disguising by screen memories and other repressive techniques the procedure and quality of its evasion — is inherently tricky, with observation subject to the same pitfalls as that which is observed. Freud explains:

> Every science is based on observations and experiences arrived at through the medium of our psychical apparatus. But since *our* science has as its subject that apparatus itself, the analogy ends here. We make our observations through the medium of the same perceptual apparatus, precisely with the help of the breaks in the sequence of 'psychical' events: we fill in what is omitted by making plausible inferences and translating it into conscious material.[9]

Thus the first 'poetic' tendency of psychoanalysis — that of being forced to use figurative language because the material to be described is uncharted and because the seeker is identical to the object of its search — is related to the second cause of this tendency: that it is a technique for filling in gaps, for creating hypotheses, for telling plausible stories. Since the aim is to study material which refuses to make itself obvious, the best approach is to note where the observable or the obvious ceases to make sense, where known explanations cease to satisfy, where normal patterns fail to indicate appropriate expectations. The mind must try to discover that it does not easily observe its own workings. Earlier, in his 1915 paper on 'The Unconscious' Freud had stated the centrality of ignorance and absence in psychoanalytic theory:

> The data of consciousness have a very large number of gaps in them; in healthy and in sick people psychical acts often occur which can be explained only by presupposing other acts, of which, nevertheless, consciousness affords no evidence. These not only include parapraxes and dreams in healthy people, and everything described as a psychical symptom or obsession in the sick; our most personal daily experience acquaints us with ideas that come into our head we do not know from where, and with intellectual conclusions arrived at we do not know how.[10]

Here psychoanalysis shows its quarry to be that of the fantasist: the aim is to catch out unexpected ignorance, thereby exposing general limitations in perception and knowledge; the limitations also reveal the strange purposes and desires of the medium of knowledge — the mind. The need to show up the gaps in a world commonly perceived as whole requires the creation of associations and patterns which utilise the representations whose strangeness is mitigated by normal inertia. The language of psychoanalysis, like the language of fantasy, is figurative but not conventionally metaphoric, since there is no means of tracing one's way back to original terms. The figurative language describes literally: only if it is so treated can its power and import be understood. But it is not scientific language; it is an attempted, even an experimental description; it provides stories to be told about mental phenomena whose very difficulty often makes them undesirable, wilfully ignored, economically discarded, requiring creative 'translation' to differentiate them and bring them to consciousness.[11]

2 Fantasy as Morality: Conrad's 'Heart of Darkness' and Hawthorne's *The Scarlet Letter*

In the great moral traditional of the novel, intellectual growth involves the shift and extension of aspects and balances. Knowledge newly gained is not knowledge of a new type but of a new arrangement. Emphases change, old interests give way to new, frequently more satisfying ones, accepted generalisations or principles are either widened or narrowed, in accord with sympathy and experience. Alternatively, new facts may be brought to light, forcing reappraisals of character and motive. The function of vividness, in relation to the moral purpose of novels within this tradition, is to turn the reader into a spectator: the reader observes character, motives, aims and situations alongside the author, and the new aspects revealed within the novel, or the more sensitive balancing suggested, form part of a general intellectual skill.

The novelists within this tradition (Jane Austen, Anthony Trollope, Mrs Gaskell, George Eliot and, to some degree, Charles Dickens and Henry James form the mainstream) work upon the premise that the moral and psychological nature of a person can be known, that behaviour over a long period and in various circumstances will confirm the validity of perceptive skills. This premise, which is to a great extent true, does not deny that such knowledge is complex, or that sensitivity and even imagination must join forces with intelligence; but it does ignore various ways in which knowledge of others and the self can lose its footing; it ignores the sense and point of various doubts as to how one knows when one has got the balance right, or whether the most important aspects have been revealed—doubts which the fantasist emphasises. Moreover, the premise ignores the question as to what type of knowledge is needed, should our common moral language suddenly seem pointless and therefore be unamenable to development.

Fantasy literature is seldom insensitive to moral questions, but at the same time it expresses profound confusion as to how to proceed towards enlightenment. The difficulty does not involve unknown facts but unknown methods of processing facts. In addition, facts lose the satisfying stability with which the realist presents them. Impressions overwhelm the mind, so that balancing becomes a balancing-out, and the number of aspects perceived leads to the vagueness of a composite image rather than to greater clarity.

Professor F.R. Leavis's criticisms of Joseph Conrad's 'Heart of Darkness' indicate the problems which the second type of moralist, the fantasist, raises. Leavis complains that whereas certain characters, events and images in Conrad's tale concretely register his theme, Conrad 'feels that there is, or ought to be, some horror, some significance he has yet to bring out'. In this attempt, Leavis sees Conrad as borrowing from the arts of the magazine writer, who in their turn have borrowed from Kipling and Poe. Conrad, he concludes, uses adjectival 'and worse than supererogatory insistence' on some undefined horror or secret for the sake of a thrilled response.[1]

The 'adjectival insistence' in 'Heart of Darkness', however, is no more than a little over-writing and leaves quite untouched the success and significance of 'some undefined horror', an emphasis which links Conrad with the fantasist and which indeed reveals the bedrock of fantasy. For here Conrad explores the blatant moral confusions underlying the European invasion of the Congo and, moreover, shows the intellect failing to tackle the confusions. The failure is due not to a special complexity, but to the refusal of moral terms to do their proper work. The traditional moralist believes that moral recognition is a basic function of human psychology. He assumes that a given body of moral truths will be acknowledged in favourable circumstances, that they can, in effect, be shown to be true. This is not to say that everyone will agree, but that a reasonably intelligent person will be compelled to acknowledge the utilitarian or intuitive force of certain arguments, even if those arguments cannot easily be made consistent. 'Heart of Darkness' shows the collapse of this assumption, with the accompanying stimulation, waywardness and exhaustion of the imagination. For where the intellect, and the crucial agreements in the area indicated by 'common sense' give way, imagination in its grotesque and groping form — the form of fantasy — dominates.

'Heart of Darkness' deals with the unsurprising moral question of what people become when social restraints are removed and what happens when an isolated society develops a moral language which condones obvious inhumanity. The narrator Marlow concludes that we must meet the challenge with our own 'inborn strength. Principles won't do.' Indeed, principles won't do because principles must be applied, and moral sensitivity is necessary to the activity of determining which cases fit the principle and which do not. However lofty, however thorough, moral principles themselves cannot ensure an acceptable morality. The white men call the natives 'enemies' or 'criminals', and therefore, according to more or less acceptable principles, a certain amout of cruelty can be justified. The intolerable treatment, therefore, is due not to the principles but to their application.

It is nonsensical to suppose that the natives are enemies or criminals, yet the consensus supports nonsense. Having heard Kurtz described in extraordinary terms, Marlow hopes for some release, through him, from the prevailing stupidity; but of course the extraordinary man is only extraordinarily evil, celebrating the moral deadness which the white officials blandly exhibit. The tale's horror rests upon the fact that no sane, stable moral point of view can be established. The homeland may seem to offer a contrasting sanity, but both the administrative offices and Kurtz's fiancée are outlandishly ignorant. The Russian whom Leavis sees as a representative of sanity is totally ironic as such a representative. He reminds Marlow of a harlequin: sanity can only be mimicked, or enacted by a clown. Marlow's conclusion is that only ignorance and illusion will preserve a belief in the possibility of morality.

The force of the tale depends upon the need to confirm a moral vision outside one's own intuitions. Marlow's voyage down the river, however inward the imagery, is not a symbolic journey into the unconscious. The uncanny impact of the journey arises from Marlow's realisation that in discovering the madness of a strange country, he also discovers a universal human madness in which he is trapped, however confidently he could state the case against it. Moral isolation is, Conrad shows, moral confusion. Thus Marlow is dumbfounded in the face of Kurtz's fiancée's faith:

'[. . .] "It is the gift of the great," she went on, and the sound of her low voice seemed to have the accompaniment of all the other sounds, full of mystery, desolation, and sorrow, I had ever heard — the ripple of the river, the soughing of the trees swayed by the wind, the murmurs of the crowds, the faint ring of incomprehensible words cried from afar, the whisper of a voice speaking from beyond the threshold of an eternal darkness. "But you have heard him! You know!" she cried.

' "Yes, I know," I said with something like despair in my heart,
but bowing my head before the faith that was in her, before that great
and saving illusion that shone with an unearthly glow in the darkness,
in the triumphant darkness from which I could not have defended her
— from which I could not even defend myself.

'[. . .] "And his example," she whispered to herself. "Men looked
up to him — his goodness shone in every act. His example —"

' "True," I said; "his example, too. Yes, his example. I forgot
that."

'[. . .] "Repeat [his last words]," she murmured in a heart-broken
tone. "I want — I want — something — something — to — to live
with."

'I was on the point of crying at her, "Don't you hear them?" The
dusk was repeating them in a persistent whisper all around us, in a
whisper that seemed to swell menacingly like the first whisper of a
rising wind. "The horror! The horror!"

'[. . .] "The last word he pronounced was — your name."[2]

The irony arises from horror: Marlow's discoveries cannot be admitted,
and so he postulates, as the only acceptable alternative, a complete
contradiction of his vision.

The moral quandary is exacerbated by the fact that it rests upon a moral
naturalism, that is, upon man's true nature. Certainly 'Heart of
Darkness' points to the release of hitherto repressed instincts: the
wilderness awakes forgotten and brutal instincts, and brings to the
memory gratified and monstrous passions;[3] but what makes this tale so
original is that the evil does not stem from desire, in any recognisable
sense of the term, but from undeniable compulsions underlying moral
blindness. The commonplace officials are hollow-natured, in that they
lack any moral responsiveness, whereas Kurtz's hollowness is an awful,
moral response to evil. Of the two nightmares Marlow chooses that of
Kurtz, not only because the man's voraciousnes gives his evil something
like a purpose, but also because he suffers in his evilness. Yet the
assurance that in his obvious soul-madness Kurtz has a soul cannot
provide consolation. His intelligence and responsiveness only serve to
activate the insubstantiality of his soul:

'[. . .] the wilderness had found him out early, and had taken on him a
terrible vengeance for the fantastic invasion. I think it had whispered
to him things about himself which he did not know, things of which
he had no conception till he took council with this great solitude —

and the whisper had proved irresistibly fascinating. It echoed loudly within him because he was hollow at the core [. . .]'[4]

It is this emptiness, not the upsurge of repressed desires, that forms the substance of Marlow's nightmare. With this discovery, there is a breakdown between desire and compulsion: there is no point — no human point — to the evil. It may be fascinating, but it is not attractive or satisfying or profound. Marlow explains:

'I've seen the devil of violence, and the devil of greed, and the devil of hot desire; but, by all the stars! these were strong, lusty, red-eyed devils, that swayed and drove men — men, I tell you. But as I stood on this hillside, I foresaw that in the blinding sunshine of that land I would become acquainted with a flabby, pretending, weak-eyed devil of a rapacious and pitiless folly.'[5]

The separation of aim and desire from compulsion undermines the struggle for life itself, so that Marlow calls the struggle with death 'the most unexciting contest you can imagine', devoid of any great desire for victory, or fear of defeat, without much belief either in one's own right or in one's adversary's.[6] Action and emotion are dissociated from the self because they are dissociated from (even unconscious) desire. The human being is dwarfed by a repulsive and aggressive natural world. His insignificance and impotence dominate him, and he flounders in a world laden with meaning, but devoid of what is normally thought to be human meaning.

In relating the tale to his companions Marlow says, 'It seems to me I am trying to tell you a dream — making a vain attempt, because no relation of a dream can convey the dream-sensation, that mingling of absurdity, surprise, and bewilderment in a tremor of struggling revolt, that notion of being captured by the incredible which is of the very essence of dreams [. . .]'[7] The emphasis on the strangeness of the experience makes Conrad stumble into assertions of 'ineffable' and 'unspeakable', but he also succeeds in conveying the elusive material. The vividness of the landscape is not a contrast to the bewilderment, but serves it in the way that perfect clarity of image increases the oddness of the dream. There is an eerie split between the passive ease of perception and the impression that meaning is both just out of reach and essential to survival. The following passage shows fantasy and vividness working together, with the images forcing home a number of moral issues that are obvious enough but impossible to grasp:

'Black shapes crouched, lay, sat between the trees leaning against the trunks, clinging to the earth, half coming out, half effaced within the dim light, in all the attitudes of pain, abandonment, and despair. Another mine on the cliff went off, followed by a slight shudder of the soil under my feet. The work was going on. The work! And this was the place where some of the helpers had withdrawn to die.

'They were dying slowly — it was very clear. They were not enemies, they were not criminals, they were nothing earthly now — nothing but black shadows of disease and starvation, lying confusedly in the greenish gloom [. . .] These moribund shapes were free as air — and nearly as thin. I began to distinguish the gleam of the eyes under the trees. Then, glancing down, I saw a face near my hand. The black bones reclined at full length with one shoulder against the tree, and slowly the eyelids rose and the sunken eyes looked up at me, enormous and vacant, a kind of blind, white flicker in the depths of the orbs, which died out slowly [. . .] While I stood horror-struck, one of these creatures rose to his hands and knees, and went off on all-fours towards the river to drink. He lapped out of his hand, then sat up in the sunlight, crossing his shins in front of him, and after a time let his woolly head fall on his breastbone.

'I didn't want any more loitering in the shade, and I made haste towards the station. When near the buildings I met a white man, in such an unexpected elegance of get-up that in the first moment I took him for a sort of vision. I saw a high starched collar, white cuffs, a light alpaca jacket, snowy trousers, a clean necktie, and varnished boots. No hat. Hair parted, brushed, oiled, under a green-lined parasol held in a big white hand. He was amazing, and had a penholder behind his ear.[8]

In one way Marlow can make sense of what he sees: the natives are dying, and they are harmless. He can also wryly describe the motives for putting them to work as 'the philanthropic desire of giving the criminals something to do'. As such, his intellect is intact, his perceptions controlled; but, at the same time, order disintegrates. 'I saw a face near my head,' shows how startlingly close these figures are, how fragmented his awareness of them, giving support to his claim that they are 'free as air — and nearly as thin'. The freedom they have is not simply the ironic freedom of being too weak to require chains, but also the ghostly freedom of moving silently through air. This ethereal quality, however, is countered by the animal crawl of the native going to the river to drink — an image itself countered immediately by the woolly head dropping on the breastbone in the pose of an abject human. Thus various horrors are compounded so quickly that Marlow's moral criticism cannot maintain its certainty. He is so shattered that the commonplace now seems impossible. The company man is untouched by the horror, and his normality further confounds Marlow: 'He was amazing, and had a penholder behind his ear.' Isolated by his awareness that what he is seeing is a nightmare, Marlow craves some confirmation of his vision in the hope of making sense of it; but the confirmation Kurtz offers only seals off all hope of confirming the sanity and morality he craves.

Marlow frequently is unable to make sense of the world on even the simple level of making out what it is that he sees. As the steamboat moves down the river the natives shoot at it. Marlow leans close to the shutter: 'and I saw a face amongst the leaves on the level with my own, looking at me very fierce and steady; and then suddenly, as though a veil had been removed from my eyes, I made out, deep in the tangled gloom, naked breasts, arms, legs, glaring eyes — the bush was swarming with human limbs in movement, glistening, of bronze colour.'[9] The landscape can suddenly become alive, but it is also unearthly in the sense of being unnatural. Just as he begins to accept strangeness as the norm, similarity strikes home and upsets the balance. Looking on to the bank from the steamer, he realises that these moving shapes are human: 'It was unearthly, and the men were — No, they were not inhuman. Well, you know, that was the worst of it — this suspicion of their not being inhuman.'[10]

Marlow is cut off from the comprehension of his surroundings, yet he is acutely responsive to them, and this combination creates the perceptual impasse that is essential to the force of fantasy:

'The living trees, lashed together by the creepers and every living bush of the undergrowth, might have been changed into stone, even to the slenderest twig, to the lightest leaf. It was not sleep — it seemed unnatural, like a state of trance. Not the faintest sound of any kind could be heard. You looked on amazed, and began to suspect yourself of being deaf — and then the night came on suddenly, and struck you blind as well.[11]

The shifting aspect of the landscape, from human to stone, the refusal of the landscape to be what Marlow would consider 'natural', is part of a world which obviously has some meaning, but whose meaning cannot be understood. 'Heart of Darkness' shows a fantasist's imagination at work in that the world it presents is close to a Symbolist's, in which external objects are terms in an abstract language; but in Conrad's work the intellect cannot function according to the Symbolist's plan; attractions themselves break apart; the world behaves like the commonplace world without making sense according to commonplace assumptions and principles. The tale concludes with Marlow's moral despair because he has experienced the instability and inefficacy of his understanding.

Fantasy grows from a moral consciousness that extends beyond shame and guilt to horror. Experiments with this extension are often made by means of demonic references and spooky effects; but in modern fantasy at its best, the extension proceeds through psychological investigation. The fantasist's reality is constructed from psychological fact.

The power of Nathaniel Hawthorne's moral vision does not stem from a subtle analysis of aims and motives or from an imaginative apprehension of consequences; instead, he creates a vision of the absolute nature of sin through which an undeniable and elusive force governs the consequences of actions. In *The Marble Faun* (1859) Hawthorne suggests that sin is a necessity for inward growth; since experience of sin discloses the profound and complex nature of humanity, it is a prelude to maturity and understanding. He fails here, however, to present a convincing interplay between sin and its consequences. The vagueness of the story — the hidden reasons for Miriam's initial guilt upon which the entire plot is based — is not due to its subtlety but to the author's refusal to let us in on the secret.

Yet Hawthorne's earlier successes in carving out the details of an intractable but elusive morality are remarkable. Judge Pyncheon's crime in *The House of Seven Gables* (1851) is similar to Bulstrode's crime in *Middlemarch* (1871-2) in that both Pyncheon and Bulstrode believe themselves to be what they appear to be in social circles; each sees himself as society would see him at his best; yet each has participated in a dishonest incident, covered up by further dishonesty, which, if revealed, would destroy his social identity. In each case, too, the author shows that the buried incidents and forgotten behaviour reveal the true character of the person, whereas his social identity hides it.

George Eliot's tale is a moral-psychological one within the realist tradition. It focusses upon the mechanisms of self-deceit and hypocrisy. She shows how hypocrisy, and a sheepish respect for one's public image, can gather momentum so that cold-blooded murder falls within a person's potential acts. George Eliot's presentation of Bulstrode's history underlines the possible ramifications of one immoral and unresolved or unpaid act. The logic employed in Bulstrode's history is a utilitarian logic: these are the consequences that can accrue from wrong actions; in this way we lose the scope of free will. She draws implications of actions within a normal and strictly human setting. Bulstrode's impasse may be modestly tragic, but it is not horrible; it has nothing of the supra-utilitarian and even supra-human influences which the fantasist brings to bear upon morality.

Hawthorne's Judge Pyncheon is not merely a respected man, nor is he merely a hypocrite. His story is not one of self-discovery or self-deceit, nor does his immorality stem from the gathering momentum of his immoral acts. These are symptoms, not the causes, of his ruthlessness. Judge Pyncheon witnessed the death of his uncle, who had a stroke as he discovered his nephew searching his rooms. He then allowed George Pyncheon to be tried, convicted and punished for his uncle's death. It is his ability to do all this with a perfectly clear conscience that gives him his awful power and which accounts for the oppression of the family house. Sin is, Hawthorne shows, a hideous force, not because it has unhappy consequences, but because it is utterly careless of consequences. It is a force that is both malevolent and unpredictable, thus creating an atmosphere of continuous anxiety and dwarfing, by malevolent egoism, everyone else's significance.

In *The House of Seven Gables,* as in 'Heart of Darkness', sin is a motivating force without particular aims: greed is an excuse, not a reason, for its exercise. Its unpredictable and undirected nature can easily be turned against the subject who exercises a sinful will. Since it is careless of consequences, it can harm anyone at all; and thus if the subject cares deeply about anyone, he can be hurt through the harm that may come to his attachment. Judge Pyncheon is himself beyond such vulnerability, but Hawthorne brings into the novel the story of Alice Pyncheon whose father allowed her to be hypnotised by Maule in return for the deed to the Eastern estates. The hypnotic spell is never broken, and at any time Maule chooses Alice may be brought under this control. His exercise of power is petty — she is made to laugh in church or to dance a jig at a funeral — yet it debars her from normal adult life.

The moral may be, as Maule tells Alice's father, 'Your daughter is destroyed because you were willing to sacrifice her to obtain the deed to the Eastern estates, to wealth and honour,' yet this is not, in fact, what Alice's father was willing to do — this was simply an unforeseen by-product of his greed. Hawthorne is not drawing a map of realistic possibilities, of plausible consequences of actions, as George Eliot does.

Rather, he is showing a malevolent power thoroughly out of control. Thus even Maule cannot dictate the consequences of his power over Alice. He makes her rush to him through the snow on his wedding day, and, as a result, Alice contracts an illness from which she dies. Maule did not want to harm her in this way; she is useless to him dead; yet the exercise of such power cannot be controlled. This is not the power that unconscious wishes have upon our will. It is linked to our knowledge that we are living in a world which is to a great extent unpredictable. Hawthorne presents sin as a special, exacerbating agent of unpredictability. He uses it to emphasise a power dissociated from will and understanding. As such, his presentation of sin is linked to a medieval fascination and fear of evil. As such, he employs a fantasist's rhetoric to reveal a human power that does not fit into an ordinary framework of desire, aim and consequence.

Hawthrone's morality is based upon his belief that, in so far as we sin, we are compelled to acknowledge a supernatural, moral presence. Thus, as we become aware of a moral reality, we lose grasp of the reality which we beheld in the simple daylight of an untroubled conscience. This assumption underlies Hawthorne's definition of the romance in his 'Preface' to *The House of Seven Gables,* where he postulates the difference between the novel and the romance as the latter's freedom to swerve from fidelity to the probable and ordinary course of man's experience, and to present human truths under strange circumstances. In the introductory sketch to *The Scarlet Letter,* 'The Custom House' (1850), Hawthorne had given a more elaborate description of the way in which the strange and uncanny serve writers' interests. Moonlight aids the sluggish imagination. Well-known details of commonplace objects

are so spiritualized by the unusual light, that they seem to lose their actual substance, and become things of intellect. Nothing is too small or too trifling to undergo this change, and acquire dignity thereby. A child's shoe; the doll, seated in her little wicker carriage; the hobby-horse —whatever, in a word, has been used or played with during the day is now invested with a quality of strangeness and remoteness, though still almost as vividly present as by daylight. Thus, therefore, the floor of our familiar room has become a neutral territory, somewhere between the real world and fairyland, where the Actual and the Imaginary may meet, and each imbue itself with the nature of the other. Ghosts may enter here without affrighting us. It would be too much in keeping with the scene to excite surprise, were we to look about us and discover a form, beloved, but gone hence, now sitting quietly in a streak of this magic moonshine, with an aspect that would make us doubt whether it had returned from afar, or had never once stirred from our fireside.

[...] Glancing at the looking glass, we behold — deep within its haunted verge — the smouldering glow of the half-extinguished anthracite, the white moonbeams on the floor, and a repetition of all the gleam and shadow of the picture, with one remove further from the actual, and nearer to the imaginative. Then, at such an hour, and with this scene before him, if a man sitting all alone cannot dream strange things and make them look like truth, he need never try to write romances.[12]

The setting Hawthorne describes is more appropriate to tales which deliberately exploit the uncanny — such as E.T.A. Hoffmann's 'Nutcracker and the King of Mice' in which Marie's night vigil reveals her toy's animation, or Colette's libretto for Ravel's opera *L'Enfant et les sortilèges* in which a young boy, confined to his room as punishment, watches his toys grow huge and menacing, thus taking on his own anger and then taking vengeance upon him for his anger — than to his own work. Moreover, in his suggestion of the plausibility, in such an atmosphere, of ghosts, he links fantasy with the supernatural, as he never does in his best fiction. It is Conrad who, in his foreword to 'The Shadow Line', which many critics read as a supernatural tale, clearly distinguishes the issues Hawthorne somewhat muddles:

I believe that if I attempted to put the strain of the Supernatural on [my imagination], it would fail deplorably and exhibit an unlovely gap. But I could never have attempted such a thing, because all my moral and intellectual being is penetrated by an invincible conviction that whatever falls under the dominion of our senses must be in nature and, however exceptional, cannot differ in its essence from all the other effects of the visible and tangible world of which we are a self-conscious part. The world of the living contains enough marvels and mysteries as it is; marvels and mysteries acting upon our emotions and intelligence in ways so inexplicable that it would almost justify the conception of life as an enchanted state. No, I am too firm in my consciousness of the marvellous to be ever fascinated by the mere supernatural, which (take it any way you like) is but a manufactured article, the fabrication of minds insensitive to the intimate delicacies of our relation to the dead and to the living, in their countless multitudes; a desecration of our tenderest memories; an outrage to our dignity.[13]

The difference, Conrad marks, is betwen an arbitrary 'other' world and our world, seen to be mysterious and marvellous: 'whatever falls under the dominion of our senses must be in nature and, however exceptional, cannot differ in its essence from all the other effects of the visible and tangible world of which we are a self-conscious part.' Our imagination, turned honestly towards the world and towards ourselves as part of the world, discovers strange and elusive phenomena which demand to be presented in a strange and elusive rhetoric. Conrad excels in revealing the natural world in relation to self-conscious perception: our experiences within the natural world are so powerful and disturbing that the understanding of natural phenomena involves the superimposition — however provisional — of a human, and moral, map upon a fantastic substance.

The supreme presentation of morality through an imagination approaching the fantastic is in Shakespeare's *Macbeth*. Macbeth's world is itself highly sensitive to moral outrage. Thus even his desires must take refuge from the observing sky: 'Stars, hide your fires! / Let not light see my black and deep desires.' But nature will register human crimes, and Macbeth's and his wife's pleas to the night to seal their deeds off are bound to fail. Initially Macbeth hopes to split up his action so that the undesired consequences will be swallowed up in the desired consequences, so that 'the eye [will] wink at the hand' as though he could bring about the desired end without actually performing the action. The morally sensitive universe, however, has a forbidding logic, which even the ruthless Lady Macbeth later perceives: she comes to suffer all those tortures of guilt which Macbeth, before the murder, feared and at which she sneered, thinking them possible to control. Macbeth himself accepts the logic of morality, and therefore embraces a horribly consistent evil.

Central to the uncanny force of morality in *Macbeth* is the tension between desire and fear, a tension which cannot be explained with a pyschoanalytic model of unconscious desire or of fear as flight before an unconscious desire, but which is linked to ways in which we learn about ourselves and our world. Macbeth and his wife see Duncan, or try to see him, merely as an obstacle to their ambition. Yet even before the murder Macbeth realises how Duncan's virtues 'Shall blow the horrid deed in every eye,' and how his being Duncan's kinsman exacerbates the evil of the crime. It is a fact of human perception and response that we cannot see people all the time as mere obstacles to our desires; and yet it is also a fact of human nature that we are apt to forget, or to neglect, those aspects of others which are not directly related to our desires. It is easy to do this when we do not know the people with whom we are dealing. It becomes more difficult, and more outrageous, when we so slight a friend or relative. Macbeth believes he might get away with disregarding (just once, he foolishly tells himself) another's full humanity; but his imagination is such that it is compelled to trace the reality of his deed.

Lady Macbeth is driven mad as she gradually sees the implications of the crime — not the practical consequences, but the implications of the act itself. She had thought herself strong enough to control morality by the suppression of compassion, but it proves itself to have a gigantic reality. In the sleep-walking scene she demands, with her former logic, 'What need we fear who knows it, when none can call our power to accompt?'. This attempt to waylay fear is countered by simple horror: 'Yet who would have thought the old man to have had so much blood in him?', and following that there is the doggerel chant, 'The thane of Fife had a wife: where is she now?' which helplessly acknowledges another's emotional loss.

Macbeth himself accepts the challenge to morality which his wife initially proposes. He accepts both the further crimes he believes necessary to maintain his position, and the grotesquely narrowed vision of others that his crimes entail. Thus, in learning of his wife's death, he understands that mourning, with its retrospective and intensified appreciation, is called for; but, given his adopted immorality, mourning has no point. The passage beginning 'She should have died hereafter' is the culminating logic of murder: if people can be viewed only in the light of one's own interests, then there is a clear sense in which they are insignificant; if one can arbitrarily — or solely in accord with one's practical, immediate interests — decide whose life is valuable and whose is not, then human life in general lacks value; and if human life in general lacks value, then one's wife's life, and even one's own, is unimportant — for it is only the mean, fighting spirit in Macbeth that makes him fight for his own.

What Macbeth's imagination perceives is a universe with a moral impact. As a result, nature is terrifying and grotesque; the defiance of the law leads to a discovery, by means familiar to the fantasist, of the uncanny force of moral law.

Hawthorne's scope is narrower than Conrad's but shares something of Shakespeare's power and purpose. He is far less adept than Conrad at presenting a natural world rich with moral meaning. Even in his best work, *The Scarlet Letter* (1850), the images of the forest, with its moral licence, versus the Christian community of the town, or of the varying fall of light and shadow, are crude indications of possible moral responses to natural phenomena; but he does succeed in thrusting moral awareness upon his characters through the discovery of their own mysterious part in a natural reality.

In *The Scarlet Letter* the reality of sin underlies life's seriousness. To acknowledge a morality based upon this reality is to grant respect to human action, however adversely judged it may be. As Hester Prynne, carrying her illegitimate daughter in her arms, stands on the scaffold in the market place:

> The scene was not without a mixture of awe, such as must always invest the spectacle of guilt and shame in a fellow-creature, before society shall have grown corrupt enough to smile, instead of shuddering, at it. The witnesses of Hester Prynne's disgrace had not yet passed beyond their simplicity. They were stern enough to look upon her death, had that been her sentence, without a murmur at its severity, but had none of the heartlessness of another social state, which would find only a theme for jest in an exhibition like the present.[14]

However misguided her judges may be in their adherence to particular moral principles (and Hawthorne declares that it would be difficult to find a body of men less capable of 'sitting in judgement upon an erring woman's heart, and disentangling its mesh of good and evil'[15]) their respect for morality, their assurance of a moral reality, is Hawthorne's own.

Fantasy in literature depends upon a peculiar, unexpected mingling of internal and external reality. (In the current British philosophical tradition, there is a general tendency to avoid using the inner/outer distinction, either because empiricism runs into grave problems if any occurrence — a mental event, for example — is, even in part, postulated as 'inner' and therefore 'private', or because — though this is now out of fashion — empiricism rejects the postulation of 'outer' objects when they can be known only be means of 'private' sensations. Nevertheless, it is easy enough to accept a division between 'inner' and 'outer' when the former refers to emotions and thoughts and the conflicts among them, and the latter refers to objects in space and to natural and human behaviour which indicate 'inner' occurrences, but which may indicate them more or less clearly). There is a special strangeness in discovering the inner world while investigating the external world (as happens in 'Heart of Darkness'), especially when this discovery occurs outside allegory, which provides rules for translating concrete images into abstractions. In *The Scarlet Letter* fantasy arises from the surprising way in which psychological and physical features mingle: inner reality is seen to have the definite outlines of external reality; emotions and emotional states, taking place within external reality, involve a second, disturbing reality with a character very much like that of the external world.

Hester feels, as she is watched and judged in the market place, that her heart has been flung into the open, to be trampled by the people's feet. This metaphor is common enough, yet such metaphors proliferate until they become the proper language for feelings. Chillingworth, in explaining to Hester his reason for marrying her while aware of her lack of love for him, says: 'My heart was a habitation large enough for many guests, but lonely and chill, and without a household fire [...] And so, Hester, I drew thee into my heart, into its innermost chamber, and sought to warm thee by the warmth which thy presence made there!'[16] The image of the heart becomes an image of a house, into which the husband literally drew the wife. Here a description of his feelings and thoughts is offered in a description of what he was doing, in the most simple, physical sense of 'action', when he married her — that is, he was taking her into his home, and his emotional actions have the same definitive outlines.

Chillingworth's approach to Dimmesdale's thoughts is as simplistically physical as his description of his marriage, but, in inner terms, it is subtle and secretive. He

> strove to go deep into his patient's bosom, delving among his principles, prying into his recollections, and probing everything with a cautious touch, like a treasure-seeker in a dark cavern [...] Then, after long search into the minister's dim interior, and turning over many precious materials in the shape of high aspirations for the welfare of his race, warm love of souls, pure sentiments, natural piety, strengthened by thought and study, and illuminated by revelation — all of which invaluable gold was perhaps no better than rubbish to the seeker — he would turn back, discouraged, and begin his quest towards another point. He groped along as stealthily, with as cautious a tread, and as wary an outlook, as a thief entering a chamber where a man lies only half asleep — or it may be, broad awake — with purpose to steal the very treasure which this man guards as the apple of his eye. In spite of his premeditated carefulness, the floor would now and then creak; his garments would rustle; the shadow of his presence, in a forbidden proximity, would be thrown across the victim. In other words, Mr. Dimmesdale, whose sensibility of nerve often produced the effect of spiritual intuition, would become vaguely aware that something

inimical to his peace had thrust itself into relation with him. But old Roger Chillingworth, too, had perceptions that were almost intuitive; and when the minister threw his startled eyes towards him, there the physician sat; his kind, watchful, sympathising, but never intrusive friend.[17]

Obviously this is a metaphorical descripton of Chillingworth's investigation but, at the same time, it leads to a literal description of his behaviour, for he does creep across the floor towards the half-sleeping Dimmesdale to uncover his bosom and to see there the 'A' which the minister has branded upon himself, thus having proof that Dimmesdale was his wife's criminal partner. The continuous, unobtrusive slide between figurative and literal language threatens the characters themselves: for if mental and emotional life is like the external world, then it can be probed ruthlessly, ignorant of its observers, and whatever is discovered can be manipulated like an external object. In the face of these possibilities private sensibilities are outraged; meticulously balanced self-judgements become violated and exposed.

Implications of this model of the mind are drawn throughout the novel. However secret the emotion, its reality is such that it will betray itself. In the most ordinary way, feelings appear in a character's behaviour, however determined he may be to conceal them. Even Chillingworth, as he sees Hester on the scaffold, must reveal his feelings, however momentarily:

A writhing horror twisted itself across his features, like a snake gliding swiftly over them, and making one little pause, with all its wreathed intervolutions in open sight. His face darkened with some powerful emotion, which, nevertheless, he so instantaneously controlled by an effort of will, that, save at a single moment, its expression might have passed for calmness.[18]

The conquering of external expression is intricately involved in Chillingworth's damnation. Inner reality, with its special link with sin, demands a hearing. The scarlet letter Hester is compelled to wear prevents her vulnerability from beccomming demonic. Her sin, because it must be acknowledged, becomes a moral asset. It gives her sympathetic knowledge of others' sins and, gradually, changes its aspect, so that, instead of a stigma, it becomes a mark to be revered.

Yet Hester's acknowledgement of her sin is far from easy, and her proud resistance to the Puritan community's judgement is so convincing that many critics have seen Hawthorne's refusal to let Hester and Dimmesdale enjoy their passion as a cowardly appendage to a brave rebellion. Clearly Hawthorne saw evil within the Puritans' harsh self-righteousness. In *The House of Seven Gables* the Pyncheons' witch-burning ancestor is linked to the hypocritical Judge Pyncheon through a history of moral and social pride and material greed; but in *The Scarlet Letter* doubts as to the foundation of the community's morality are firmly countered within the novel. Hester's uncertainty as to the validity of the sympathetic information the scarlet letter provides is uncertainty as to how her anger against the community influences her thoughts. Her anxiety about her daughter's nature is anxiety about the logic of sin: can good come from an evil deed? The child's playful and manipulating ambivalence, which teases Hester's doubts as to whether she deserves affection, are seen by mother as the mark of the Devil. However bold she seems to be, her challenge to Dimmesdale to reject the community's judgement cannot be sustained within the network of her beliefs. If it is merely the feeling of guilt that Hawthorne expounds, if, as many critics have alleged, he did not believe that Hester and Dimmesdale had truly sinned and that one should rejoice in Dimmesdale's fall from such false beliefs,[19] then the guilty mind nonetheless creates its own reality, with sin at the centre.

Hester's entire being is defined in relation to her sin, and she does not resist this definition. She could escape from the community; she could return to England, or leave Boston for another part of America, but her 'sin, her ignominy were the roots which she had struck into the soil.'[20] Her sin changes her relationships and her duties: the 'links that united her to the rest of human kind — links of flowers, or silk, or gold, or whatever the material — had all been broken. Here was the iron link of mutual crime, which neither he nor she could break.'[21] The 'iron link' has nothing to do with the compensatory retribution of a utilitarian morality, but is a result of the profound, original dimension sin discloses. Her only hope for peace is to find a path within this strange and awesome world, to accept the laws which govern it. Her somewhat meek compliance is indeed disappointing, but Hawthorne has shown that even Hester's strength cannot resist moral reality.

Since sin is undeniable, the attempt to hide it involves not only frantic watchfulness but also a violation of one's fundamental being. The strange objectivity of sin is linked to the externality of the human mind, to the frequent images of the mind or heart as a place that can be explored as a physical place can be explored. Chillingworth counts upon this when he challenges Hester's declaration that he will never learn the father of her child:

'Never, sayest thou?' rejoined he, with a smile of dark and self-relying intelligence. 'Never know him! Believe me, Hester, there are few things—whether in the outward world, or, to a certain depth, in the invisible sphere of thought — few things hidden from the man who devotes himself earnestly and unreservedly to the solution of a mystery . . .'

The eyes of the wrinkled scholar glowed so intensely upon her that Hester Prynne clasped her hands over her heart, dreading lest he should read the secret there at once.[22]

'The invisible sphere of thought' will project itself upon the visible. For one intent upon reading its appearance upon the visible world, success will come. The inner world has a compulsion to reveal itself, and to resist this compulsion is to ally oneself with the Devil. The result is not only anxiety at one's untenable task, but an infective confusion. As soon as Dimmesdale appears Hawthorne introduces the moral irony which runs throughout the novel; expression, given the demonic denial of the inner — that is, moral — self, is counter to genuine meaning, however much the subject may wish to offer genuine expression. As the young pastor speaks to Hester, who stands on the scaffold, his

> voice was tremulously sweet, rich, deep, and broken. The feeling that it so evidently manifested, rather than the direct purport of the words, caused it to vibrate within all hearts, and brought the listeners into one accord of sympathy. Even the poor baby at Hester's bosom was affected by the same influence, for it directed its hitherto vacant gaze towards Mr. Dimmesdale, and held up its little arms, with a half pleased, half plaintive murmur. So powerful seemed the minister's appeal, that the people could not believe but that Hester Prynne would speak out the guilty name; or else the guilty one himself, in whatever high or lowly place he stood, would be drawn forth by an inward and inevitable necessity, and compelled to ascend the scaffold.[23]

The irony here is easily enough unwound: the baby turns to the voice of her father, not to the voice of God, and the tremulousness of the voice is not of the angels but of human shame. Always, because he hides his sin, Dimmesdale's behaviour is deceptive. He tries to tell the people that he is guilty, but in speaking 'the very truth' he 'transformes it into the veriest falsehood'. The hypocrisy of his pious position confounds the people's piety: 'The virgins of his church grew pale around him, victims of a passion so imbued with religious sentiment that they imagined it to be all religion, and brought it openly, in their white bosoms, as their most acceptable sacrifice before the altar.'[24]

The split between the inner truth of sin and its public denial is the Devil's triumph. However isolated Hester is by her shame, Dimmesdale is more isolated by his secret guilt. He mounts the scaffold alone, at night, in a mockery of self-effacement, and wonders what would happen if the people of Boston were to discover him there. He imagines them, in their excitement, rushing from their homes in their nightclothes. The most respectable would appear the most ridiculous: 'Carried away by the grotesque horror of this picture, the minister, unawares, and to his own infinite alarm, burst into a great peal of laughter.'[25] His knowledge of his own hypocrisy makes everyone else seem hypocritical. Since his own pretensions are ridiculous, everyone's seem so. Again, returning to the town after his meeting in the forest with Hester, the moral atmosphere is changed by the recent confrontation with his secret self. The alienation from his social identity emerges as a demonic urge towards gleeful denigration: 'At every step he was incited to do some strange, wild, wicked thing or other, with a sense that it would be at once involuntary and unintentional; in spite of himself, yet growing out of a profounder self than that which opposed the impulse.'[26]

The attempt to deny sin creates a rent in the natural order of which sin is a part, but it is even more dangerous to meddle, as Chillingworth does, with the complex relation between a person and his guilt. Just as the Puritan community reveals an ugly and evil aspect in its judgement of Hester, even though the content of the judgement may be correct, Chillingworth becomes grotesque in his pursuit of justice. Throughout his life he had been

calm in temperament, kindly, though not of warm affections, but ever, and in all relations with the world, a pure and upright man. He had begun an investigation, as he imagined, with the severe and equal integrity of a judge, desirous only of truth, even as if the question involved no more than the air-drawn lines and figures of a geometrical problem, instead of human passions and wrongs inflicted upon himself. But, as he proceeded, a terrible fascination, a kind of fierce, though still calm, necessity seized the old man within its grip and never set him free again, until he had done all its bidding. He now dug into the poor clergyman's heart like a miner searching for gold; or, rather like a sexton delving into a grave, possibly in quest of a jewel that had been buried in the dead man's bosom, but likely to find nothing save mortality and corruption. Alas for his own soul, if these were what he sought![27]

A person's thoughts are as solid and enduring as external objects, but they are also far more complex and delicate. Thus, to approach another's inner self ruthlessly is to meddle with the mystery of human experience, which is of course to meddle with the mystery of sin. In so doing one assumes the Devil's work and becomes a devil one's self. Chillingworth, with his awful understanding, tells Hester that his constant infliction of suffering upon Dimmesdale has actually increased, not mitigated, the harm done to himself: he has become evil through the pursuit of justice, and so the effects of the initial sin are compounded. Moreover, Chillingworth is bound to his evil task. His hatred of the minister makes him as dependent upon him as love would: a passionate hater is as forlorn without the object of his passion as is a passionate lover.[28] The man who interfered in the delicate mystery of sin, who was deceived by its order and purpose into thinking it could be approached objectively, becomes enmeshed within it, understanding its laws but powerless against them.

Hawthorne admired the novelists in the realist tradition. He envied Trollope's ability to carve out a piece of reality and present it in fiction, yet he acknowledged his own compulsion to investigate that area where the 'Actual and Imaginary may meet'. His insistence upon the physical characteristics of the inner world can be seen as an allegorist's epilogue to the Gothic tale, in which the sacred has degenerated into haunting apparitions, or it can be seen as a prelude to a psychoanalytic study of guilt, with the father's sternness exaggerated within the Oedipal gloom. Yet Hawthorne's work, like Conrad's, shows that the sacred extends to the natural plane. He presents a world transformed by psychology — not re-interpreted, not represented, but elusively and frighteningly transformed; and, to survive, we must understand the forces thereby revealed. Human perception and fear create moral laws; our creations are our reality — and this recognition forms the bedrock of fantasy.

3 The Uncanny: Freud, E.T.A. Hoffmann, Edgar Allan Poe

Freud's paper 'The Uncanny'[1] is the best essay on the subject. It was written in 1919, when he was also working on *Beyond the Pleasure Principle,* and it shares with that work a new breadth of vision. Previously Freud's ingenuity had been directed to the task of explaining what pleasure was to be gained, or what pain avoided, from behaviour that appeared to have no motive, or that disguised its motive. In addition, his task was to show that however bizarre the behaviour, pleasure was pursued (or pain avoided) in the most economical manner possible, given the divisions and tensions within the mind. Now, in acknowledging the repetition compulsion, Freud identified a principle of mental functioning which defied the pleasure principle.

The repetition principle is 'beyond' the pleasure principle in two senses. First, it is prior to it but does not contradict it: the mind works over—or endeavours to work over — some original impression in order to master its evocative anxiety and thereby convert the tension into pleasure. Secondly, the repetition principle is actually inconsistent with the pleasure principle: it is an effort to restore a psychic state that is developmentally primitive and marked by the drainage of energy in accord with the death instinct. This recognition led Freud to revise the assumption that two fundamental, and related, sets of instincts were at work: libidinal and self-preservative, which subsequently were suggested to be only libidinal, since self-preservation could be classified as a libidinal instinct by describing it as the libido directed towards the self. He now postulated a second duality of instincts, the libidinal and death instincts. The death instinct was defined as the impulse to return to a prior developmental phase — the inorganic state; and this instinct could take on an aggressive drive when it was deflected from the self on to others.

Beyond the Pleasure Principle stands out in Freud's writings as his most overtly speculative and poetic vision, yet the repetition compulsion supposed to be at the basis of the death instinct and its link to traumatic dreams, to games and to art became the bedrock of Freud's later theories. The mind had to protect itself from stimuli; repetition was an attempt to reduce the level of excitation in ideas or emotions; it was a means of preparation, allowing the psyche to meet challenges or surprises in a comfortable low key. How strange, then, that the principle of repetition should become the means by which Freud explains that literature which so clearly aims at increasing excitement and surprise and confusion.

Freud begins the essay on the uncanny with his customary apology for broaching aesthetic matters by saying that psychoanalysis 'has little to do with the subdued emotional impulses which, inhibited in their aims and dependent upon a host of concurrent factors, usually furnish the material for the study of aesthetics.'[2] He declares, therefore, that he will treat only a neglected and remote aspect of the aesthetics of the uncanny. As is also his custom, he proceeds, ignoring his diffident approach, to discuss the subject as a whole. He asks what it is that distinguishes the uncanny from the fearful or, rather, how it can be defined as a special class of the fearful. The uncanny, he concludes, belongs to that class of the terrifying which leads back to something long known by us or felt by us: in short, the uncanny, or strange, actually points to the recurrence of something very familiar, but repressed or discarded.

The German word Freud is considering is *unheimlich* — literally unhomely, unfamiliar; but it can also mean the opposite — secret, hidden. For that which is familiar to oneself, or belonging to one's home, can be hidden from others and therefore secret, unfamiliar and strange (e.g., private parts). The ambiguity of meaning indicates the type of familiarity and the type of strangeness the term is used to describe, and emphasises the reason for the strangeness: the prefix 'un-' is the sign for repression.

Freud continues the study of uncanny phenomena with a discussion of E.T.A. Hoffmann's 'The Sand-Man' and in so doing provides one of his most satisfying discussion of a literary work in which psychoanalytic biography, often grossly speculative and psychologically naïve,[3] is reduced to a suggestive coda. Freud believes that Nathanael's uncertainty as to Olympia's status — whether she is a mannikin or a woman — is derived from the child's supposition that dolls are alive; and though this supposition may be based upon wish or desire rather than fear, the fact that it is a discarded belief or fantasy which later recurs, renders it uncanny. Freud believes, however, that this theme is incidental to the tale and far less striking than the central notion of having one's eyes plucked out.

It is known that this can be a terrible childhood fear; and a study of dreams, fantasies and myths, Freud believes, shows that a morbid anxiety connected with eyes, going blind or losing one's eyes is often a substitute for the dread of castration. Thus Oedipus' self-blinding can be understood as a means of carrying out a mitigated form of the punishment of castration, the punishment suitable to the crime of making love to his mother. It is the dread of castration, also, which explains Nathanael's horror at the sand-man, who tears out children's eyes. Only if the eyes are understood as a substitute for the male genitalia, Freud maintains, does the structure of the story make sense. For Hoffmann connects the anxiety about eyes with the father's death: it is the wish for the father's death, associated with the desire to possess the mother, that brings about the fear of retribution with castration. The close association of Coppelius with the father represents two images constructed by the child's ambivalence: the avenging father who tries to tear out Nathanael's eyes, and the loving father who intercedes for him. That part of the castration complex which is most strongly repressed — the death-wish against the father — finds expression in the death of the good father, which is attributed to the bad father. Each time the sand-man (or his surrogates) appears, he separates Nathanael from his object choice. The conjunction of events is intelligible, Freud believes, only when the sand-man is seen as the dreaded father who will castrate the son. The uncanny effect of the sand-man is a result of the child's projection of dread.

Freud's discussion of 'The Sand-Man' is distinctly psychoanalytic, as opposed to psychological; that is, it proffers an explanation of the drama and its images in terms of unconscious material. In the process one set of terms is replaced by another. The protagonist seems to be concerned with fear about his eyes and about his father's death; but, psychoanalytically interpreted, all this is seen to be about something else — not in the way an allegory tells one story which, given literary conventions for inter-pretation, provides a scheme of ideas, but as a thief might use a disguise; substitutions are sneaked in, and their secrecy is subtley preserved. (In contrast, Freud's essay on the *Moses* of Michelangelo is psychological rather than psychoanalytic. It deals with aspects of the sculpture that can be read off from it, not into it. Moses' posture is studied; the appearance is studied; the aim is to discover the implications of the appearance and to relate it to the normal framework of action and motive. The essay is a highly satisfying attempt to place the statue's pose in the context of an action which expresses rather than disguises its meaning.)

In his psychoanalytic interpretation of Hoffmann's tale, Freud uses 'The Sand-Man' as a model for another story. He treats the author's tale as the manifest content of a latent tale, in the way that the dream one has, or the dream one relates is only the manifest content of the latent (true) dream thoughts, transformed by the dream-work in which the censor plays a strong part. Thus the images the author employs — the fear of losing one's eyes and horror at the father's death — are replaced by psychoanalytic images, by the male member, fear of castration, and guilt at the death-wish towards the father. The psychoanalytic tale severely limits the range of possible references. Eyes no longer have the wealth of association the author seems to provide, for such associations are irrelevant to the substituted term and substituted story. How else can the tale be read?

Lothar and his sister Clara are orphans who come to live with Nathanael and his mother (who are their distant relations) after the death of Nathanael's father. Nathanael becomes engaged to Clara before going to the university. While he is living in the university town he meets a pedlar of optical equipment. The meeting disturbs him, for he identifies the pedlar as the man responsible for his father's death. He writes to Lothar, telling him the story of his father's death and that he feels, because of this death, that some awful fate awaits him.

In Nathanael's narration there are constant references to eyes and to seeing. He and his brothers and sisters saw little of their father during the day. His father told him many wonderful stories and got so excited that his pipe went out, and Nathanael's chief amusement was to light it for him. At other times the father would give the children picture books to look at while he sat puffing such great clouds of smoke that they were enveloped in a mist. Thus the father offers the children both frustration and delight in regard to visual pleasure: they do not see him during the day, and when they do see him, he stimulates their visual pleasure with picture books, and then frustrates them again by puffing clouds of smoke which impede their vision.

On evenings when he thus frustrates the children, he is silent and the mother seems sad. She tells the children that they must go to bed, because the sand-man is coming. When Nathanael asks his mother about the sand-man she says that the phrase, 'the sand-man is coming', simply means that the children are sleepy and cannot keep their eyes open, as though someone had thrown sand into their eyes; but the old woman who nurses his youngest sister tells him that the sand-man is a wicked man who, when children refuse to go to bed, throws handfuls of sand in their eyes, making the eyes jump out of the children's heads, and that he then puts the bloody eyes into a bag which he gives to his little ones on the half-moon where, with hooked beaks like owls, they pick at the children's eyes.

Thus far a psychoanalytic tale distinct from, though not in contradiction to the one Freud suggests, is a good candidate for interpretation. The dreaded night brings on the parents' love-making (which, from the mother's sadness, it would seem she dreaded, whereas the father's preoccupation might be threatening). The children are forbidden to witness the activity — thus the smoke from their father's pipe clouds their vision, and thus it is the bad father, Coppelius, Nathanael hears climbing the stairs when he is in bed: this is the father who will engage in sexual activity and it is this father upon whom Nathanael wishes to spy, and it is for this wish he will be punished by blindness. As with Freud's interpretation, however, this account of the given material does not make sense if taken as the true material of the tale; it simply offers suggestions for a story to tell alongside part of the author's story.

Nathanael knows the nurse's description of the sand-man cannot be true, yet he is terrified; and at the same time, he loves to dwell upon the story of the sand-man. He scribbles his picture everywhere in extraordinary and repulsive forms. He tries to catch sight of Coppelius who, however, closes the door before Nathanael can get a look. One evening he conceals himself in the father's study. He sees Coppelius hammer something he has taken out of the fire. Nathanael believes that these molten pieces are men's eyeless faces, and when Coppelius cries, 'Eyes here! Eyes here!' (presumably catching sight of the child spy) Nathanael screams. Coppelius declares that he wants to take out Nathanael's eyes but desists as the father pleads for his son, adding, 'but we will at any rate examine the mechanism of the hand and foot.'

Freud points out that Coppelius here treats Nathanael as a manikin, thus identifying him with Olympia, the manikin with whom Nathanael falls in love. This is an apt, suggestive and even exciting point, but when he then declares that Olympia, the automatic doll, 'can be nothing else than a materialisation of Nathanael's feminine attitude towards his father in his infancy' and that she is 'as it were, a dissociated complex of Nathanael's which confronts him as a person, and Nathanael's enslavement to this complex is expressed in his senseless obsessive love for Olympia,' a love which can be called narcissitic and which explains why 'he who has fallen victim to it should relinquish his real, external object of love,'[4] the door to interesting interpretation is closed. Freud is not exactly guilty of the confusion of applying a type of analysis to a literary character that can only be justly applied to a patient (whose acceptance of the analysis is crucial to the determination of its truth), for he is relating Nathanael's case to actual cases; but he forces upon us a tenor of the metaphor (for which the tale is the vehicle) that in effect deflects more subtle interpretations. Certainly Nathanael's love for Olympia is narcissistic, and his need for the manikin marks his intolerance of Clara, 'his real, external object of love', but Nathanael's battle is against the impediments and confusion of vision in a very broad sense; his anxiety, and the uncanniness to which it subjects him, is turned into a gross comedy by Freud's insistence that it is the dread of castration. Why must Freud's story be *the* story? To appeal to his theory about which instincts are fundamental, is both circular and insufficient, for it is far from clear that a 'fundamental' instinct cannot undergo such transformation that analysis into its primitive components is not only irrelevant but virtually nonsensical.

Let us, for the moment, continue with the tale. Nathanael, having been threatened by Coppelius and saved by his father (one could postulate, as a realistic version of Nathanael's horror story, a cruel game Coppelius was playing, with the father joining in both nervously and insensitively), loses consciousness. When he awakes he is being comforted by his mother, who assures him that the sand-man is no longer there. Coppelius, however, does return, and when the mother grows pale, the father tells her this will be his last visit. During this visit there is an explosion in the study. Nathanael's father dies with his face horribly blackened and burnt.

Nathanael tells Lothar that the pedlar who visited him is Coppelius, though he now calls himself 'Guiseppe Coppola' ('Coppo' in Italian is 'eye-socket'). Clara, who reads the letter addressed to her brother, explains that his mother's sadness stems from the fact that his father and Coppelius (i.e., 'crucible') were engaged in alchemical practices which drained the family income. Her bland reasonableness (Nathanael has teased her for her cool-headedness, and the emptiness of her vision is borne out by Nathanael's belief that her eyes reflect only the sea and sky) sets Nathanael on edge; for however truly she may speak, her advice — basically, to get a hold of himself — denies the reality of his fears and of his need to pin his vision to that darker power. Thus Nathanael petulantly misinterprets her: 'She has written me a very deep philosophical letter, proving conclusively that Coppelius and Coppola only exist in my own mind and are phantoms of my own self, which will at once be dissipated, as soon as I look upon them in that light.'[5] She has admitted that these figures, or their threatening aspect, are reflections of his self; what she therefore denies is the reality of that self.

When he and Clara are together again, and when it seems that they may be happy with each other, he reads her his poem in which he describes the two of them standing by the altar, where they are interrupted by Coppelius, who touches Clara's eyes. Her eyes leap into Nathanael's breast, 'burning and hissing like bloody sparks'. Clara (in Nathanael's poem) assures him that her eyes are unharmed, but when he turns to her in relief, he sees her cast death's gaze upon him. The poem is a good, dynamic fantasy. It reveals his belief that Clara is both actively hostile to him and that her calmness is deathly: she wants to destroy him, and will destroy him through even her kind intentions. Nathanael is inclined to deny the anger reflected in the poem: 'Whose hideous voice is this?' he screams as he reads the poem, yet when Clara advises him to throw the useless, senseless thing into the fire, he calls her a 'lifeless automaton'. He accuses her of being what Olympia actually is because she denies his reality, whereas he fantasises Olympia's reality because, he believes, she acknowledges his. His confusion and doubt are such that only from something worse than blindness, only from the absolute non-seeing of a manikin, can he trust a 'response'.

Nathanael fears that his clumsy attempts to express his thoughts will make his own thoughts seem cold and dead even to himself. To convince himself of their validity, he must persuade others to see them. Eyes and vision play a significant role in his attachment to Olympia, though his vision — and he knows this — is always going wrong: the fear of being unable to distinguish among perception, fear and desire is central to the uncanny effect.

It is as a voyeur that Nathanael first sees Olympia. Climbing the stairs to Spalanzani's flat, he peers through an incompletely closed curtain and sees the doll. Initially he is disturbed by her eyes, which seem to have no power of vision; but later, after his lodgings have been burned in a chemist's accident, he moves to a house opposite Spalanzani's and, using the pedlar's glass to spy on the manikin, sees passion and love in her eyes. The pedlar's glass, he believes, brings things out sharply and distinctly; but of course, what he sees clearly and distinctly is false. Though many people are fooled into thinking Olympia is alive, only Nathanael is deceived about her inner nature: the others call her 'Miss Wax-Face' and laugh at his infatuation. As a sign of his devotion, he brings her a ring given him by his mother, but when he arrives he finds Coppola and Spalanzani fighting over the manikin. Coppola runs away with it, and Spalanzani exhorts Nathanael to run after him on the grounds that the doll's eyes are Nathanael's own. When Spalanzani throws the doll's bloodied eyes at Nathanael, he is struck with madness, crying, as he tries to strangle the professor, 'Aha! Aha! Aha! Fire-wheel — fire-wheel! Spin round, fire-wheel! Merrily, merrily! Aha! Wooden doll!' He recovers from this episode and confirms his engagement to Clara. As they are walking in the town they are about to leave, she suggests they go up to the tower of the town hall to have a last look. Nathanael takes out his eye-glass and in the distance sees Coppola approaching the market. Crying, 'Spin round, wooden doll!', he tries to throw Clara from the tower, but she is saved by her brother, and Nathanael throws himself to the street below.

There is no doubt that Freud's reading proliferates meanings according to its own references. The blood on Olympia's eyes might be due to a wound Spalanzani received in the scuffle, but it might also point to the connection with castration — a wound from which there would obviously be blood. Also, it would explain why Olympia's eyes, with their blood, seemed to belong to Nathanael. The fact that he brings Olympia a ring belonging to his mother might indicate his (vaginal) identification of Olympia and his mother and thus would explain, in the Oedipal model, the ensuing image of castration. The boldness and ingenious coherence of Freud's theory-laden interpretation is difficult to ignore. It gives the impression of certainty and clarity; but if it is extended, the clarity becomes a severe limitation. Freud acknowledges that Hoffmann persuades the reader to look, along with Nathanael, through Coppola's glasses, that he does not allow the reader to look upon the madman's imagination with the superiority of a rational mind; yet the psychoanalyst tries to uncover and avoid the very traps Hoffmann's tale sets for us, and for that reason reduces and eliminates the problems much in the same way as Clara does when she interprets or explains Nathanael's responses. The objection is not that Nathanael's responses and constructions do not have a sexual nature, or even that they do not have the sexual character and aim Freud imputes to them. Rather, it is that Freud's reading does not, as it purports, provide an answer to the puzzling text. For even if we were to accept his interpretation, questions would remain as to the nature of the mind that constructs such meanings, or the terror involved in such constructions, forcing Nathanael, when he realises that his mind continues to work in this way, to commit suicide. Freud's hypotheses about the aims and meanings of Nathanael's fantasies are, as I have said, limited, but, more importantly, they ignore the terror within the ambiguity itself. Nathanael's real tragedy is that he cannot test reality, and he cannot test it because his perceptions constantly slide from meaning to meaning and from affect to affect. Freud's story might correspond to one stage in the slide, but it would not supply an analysis of Nathanael's problem. Appeal to the theory of over-determination (i.e., that one image or idea may arise from a multitude of thoughts) will not help the psychoanalytic critic to acknowledge the tale's properly fantastic rhetoric, because the theory does not undermine the definite outlines of the central psychoanalytic story, but merely allows that a wide, undetermined range of causes gave rise to the story.

Let us recall Freud's account of the uncanny: a repetition compulsion in the unconscious, strong enough to overrule the pleasure principle, is at work, and whatever reminds us of this, is perceived as uncanny. For every affect, when repressed, is transformed by repression into anxiety. (Freud subsequently postulated anxiety as precedent and giving rise to repression, not, as here, resulting from repression: but this change would not necessarily influence his theory of uncanny phenomena.) Among such types of anxiety there is a class in which anxiety stems from what is repressed but which also recurs. This class of morbid anxiety determines what is uncanny, whether the repressed belief or emotion originally aroused dread or some other affect. The discarded belief or the repressed idea might originally have aroused pleasure: the notion of a living doll is uncanny, even though one originally derived pleasure from the belief that one's doll was real.

After discussing 'The Sand-Man' in terms of the (concealed) recurring castration fear, Freud considers how other instances of the uncanny are explained by his theory. The involuntary repetition of actions or events which gives the impression of the inevitable, hearkens back to the notion of the omnipotence of thought. This belongs to the narcissistic stage of human development, and to the primitive animistic conception of the universe. These beliefs in the power of mind to make its thoughts immediately and even unintentionsally effectual are gradually replaced by the reality principle; but when the laws of reality are ignored, when primitive beliefs are stirred, an uncanny effect is achieved.

The uncanniness of the blurred distinction between imagination and reality, or of imagination coming to life, is closely allied to the primitive belief in the omnipotence of thought. Also, it is allied to the over-accentuation of psychic reality, and an inability to trust one's apprehension of reality. The uncanny quality of ghost stories stems from the fact that in regard to death and to dead bodies our present beliefs and fears retain their primitive character. For a similar reason madness appears uncanny, as does psychoanalysis, which uncovers hidden, primitive human forces.

Thus Freud's theory degenerates into little more than a tautology. To say that the uncanny deals with themes about which we tend to feel uncertain is to make a point of only minor and certainly not surprising interest. The supposition that 'primitive' or 'archaic' beliefs and desires are involved is a modest enough supposition about any confusion, but Freud adds to it a theory about their being aroused as the result of a repetition compulsion. If this is so, then the function and logic of this compulsion need to be explained. Freud does so in terms of the death instinct — there is a compulsion to return to an earlier, that is, inorganic, state of being — or the need to master a situation which previously caught us off guard.[6] But the system of mastery is, in Freud's view, little more than a hammering away at an idea, getting used to it, reducing its power to stimulate us, whereas the function of uncanny material in literature — the function it has at its best — is to get things right, to investigate the confusions, or to reveal unexpected or ignored confusions. Freud misses this because he emphasises the arousal of primitive and repressed material; and arousal of confusing and frightening material does not necessarily involve the same kind of work that investigation or portrayal of such material involves. Thrillers, ghost stories and science fiction appeal to the desire to have such feelings aroused; in this appeal can be seen the craving to stimulate a neglected fear or desire. But arousal is not enough. The legitimate excitement must give way to exploration.

Freud acknowledges that many themes he lists as uncanny occur in literature without making an uncanny effect. This, he believes, is due to the writer's ability to create his own conditions of reality. In fairy tales ordinary reality is abandoned, and therefore the use of discarded beliefs does not conflict with the established norm. Yet even when the writer establishes his world as ours, Freud's listed themes may occur without uncanny effect. In Ibsen's *The Master Builder,* for example, Solness is disturbed by the fact that people seem to guess his wishes and act in accord with them. Also, he is disturbed by the fact that luck is on his side — or, rather, that the most awful things happen so that he can get what he wants. His wife's family home is burnt down, and though this is virtually a crippling tragedy for her (leading, somewhat indirectly, to the death of his infant sons as well), it provides him with the opportunity to build on the razed land. Even when he learns that the fire could not have been caused by his neglect, he believes that the fire was his fault, that his knowledge that the destruction of the house would help his career, caused the house to burn. Here are several themes listed by Freud as uncanny — repetition of events brought about by factors outside one's will, the power of thought alone to shape events, and the ruthless vengeance following the immediate fulfilment of wishes in the death of his sons and his wife's despair over the loss of the family home and possessions.

Solness, not surprisingly, fears that people will think him mad; the significant events in his life are shaped as fantasy would shape them. Yet in Ibsen's play, these themes are not uncanny, nor do they belong to the rhetoric of fantasy. *The Master Builder* is a psychological — not, as many critics have maintained, a symbolist — drama. Solness's fears, and the basis upon which his guilt rests, can be clearly demarcated; the question of their rationality or truth can be answered. His mistaken beliefs become excuses for selfish or cruel action, according to recognisable psychological principles; they do not, as would such mistakes in fantasy, transform the nature of perception and psychology.

Fantasy teases the mind with the way in which it can surprise and confound itself. Uncanny effects srike upon the fascination of confusion and doubt. It is arbitrary to relate the uncanny to the arousal of repressed material, for in fact the uncanny touches upon material that is frequently ignored because it is too elusive to fit into the normal framework of thought — elusive not because the material is unwanted but because it is unstable, incoherent and indefinite. Freud is correct in saying that madness has links with the uncanny in that both exhibit the domination of mental life over physical reality; but the latter, in good fantasy literature, does not deny reality for the sake of personal wishes and fears, whether conscious or unconscious, but presents in that domination truths about perception, belief, fear and desire. 'The Sand-Man' is a tale about a madman, but the psychoanalytic account of his madness not only ignores but excludes the central thrust of the story: vision confounded by fear and desire, normal reference points abolished, with ensuing isolation and despair. The need for understanding is as fundamental, surely, as the Oedipus complex, and the ever-present possibility of failure can bring with it as many terrors.

Psychoanalytic interpretations are not always thrust upon literature by the theorist, but often enlisted by the critic. They may seem required because the effect of a work is both very strong and not easily accounted for: Mozart's music may evoke as powerful a response as that of Wagner, but whereas the former's power is seen to stem from its beauty and expressiveness, there is some extra cause in Wagner's case, a cause linked to his controversiality, to the aversion he is likely to evoke and which is comprehensible to his admirers, whereas such aversion to Mozart would be incomprehensible. It is not clear that the psychoanalytic interpreter can always help us in such cases, but some explanation outside the realm of ordinary references and recognitions is needed. Henry James exploits the peculiar power of unaccountable effects in 'The Turn of the Screw', which has, unsurprisingly, given rise to a plethora of psychoanalytic interpretations. The impulse is to make explicit that which depends upon interlocking and often unstable associations, or to offer a theoretical accont of 'atmosphere', thereby denying the very suggestiveness which gives the work its value. In this fashion the psychoanalytic critic undermines the work of the literary critic who maps a wealth of meanings, but who may, in laziness and confusion, seek a single answer.

Psychoanalytic interpretation may also appeal to the critic in cases where the drama's motivation lies outside the more obvious terms offered within the work. Tennessee Williams's *Cat on a Hot Tin Roof* is about mendacity and hypocrisy, but Brick's resistance to these does not explain his sexual reconciliation with his wife, and if the play's conclusion is seen to be valid, then some other explanation must be sought, an explanation involving the sexual nature of his reconciliation with his father and the basis of his hatred for the woman who, he believes, made love to Springer (which was obviously what he himself wanted to do). In this light the conclusion is much less simplistic, since his homosexual desires are not obliterated but merely removed from competition with his wife.

In these examples psychoanalysis can illuminate aspects of the work or its effects, though a large part of its meaning is clear without reference to it. Yet psychoanalytic theory generally aims at more thorough re-interpretations, and there are cases in which even this extreme approach is welcome. Edgar Allan Poe stands out as a writer committed to the presentation of madness in bizarre images that prove particularly tempting to Freud's followers. The power of Poe's writing lies in its compulsion towards the gruesome, alongside a sadism that aspires to glamour without diminishing disgusting details. The apparent gratuitousness of the thrilling awfulness seems to demand psychoanalytic explanation: another story must be told alongside Poe's own to make sense of it.

Ambiguity, incompleteness and unexplained effects offer invitations to psychoanalytic interpretation. When abnormality and perversion join forces with them, the invitation is extended to a cry for help. Poe's grotesque images feel symbolic, and a Gothic eroticism pervades his imagination, so that analytic interpretations, which also have this characteristic, seem suitable. The quality of his symbols is such that a sexual interpretation and theoretical filling-in satisfy, answer the problems raised by the tales. This very satisfaction indicates their poverty: the interpretation that deprives the language of its fantastic impetus, improves the tale. The appropriateness of psychoanalytic interpretation to Poe's work, and the difference between Poe's work and other fantasy tales (Hoffmann's, for example) may indicate the limits of such interpretations. Marie Bonaparte's detailed study of Poe's work according to psychoanalytic theory is a classic example of such criticism.[7] Though she indulges in the confusions common to such interpreters (e.g., identifying characters strictly as composites of Poe's relatives, passing directly from analysis of a character's psychology to analysis of Poe's, using a tale to support a psychoanalytic supposition by describing the tale in psychoanalytic terms), her study exhibits the peculiar magic of analytic interpretations which can stop other criticism dead, partly by the intimidating crudeness of the terms substituted for the story's terms and of the method of substitution, and partly by the comic ingeniousness of the entire process. Berenice's teeth, in Poe's tale about a man obsessed with the possession of his dead lover's teeth, become tools for castration according to the following rationale: the mouth is a substitute for the vagina, which is imagined to have teeth by many men suffering from impotence (and their impotence is caused by this fantasy). The substitution of one term for another needs only to be suggested to remain final. On the basis of the substitution, interpretation proceeds along theoretical lines:

> when Egaeus yields to the morbid impulse to draw Berenice's teeth, he yields both to the yearning for the mother's organ and to be revenged upon it, since the dangers that hedge it about make him sexually avoid all women as too menacing. His act is therefore a sort of retributive castration inflicted on the mother whom he loves, and yet hates, because obdurate to his sex-love for her in his infancy.[8]

And in Bonaparte's analysis of 'The Fall of the House of Usher' the fissure that runs from the top to the bottom of the house recalls the cloven body of the woman. Once this similarity has been drawn, the house is seen to be the woman, the dead and avenging mother who seizes Usher-Poe from beyond the grave (for the house is Madeline's double, who is automatically identified with the mother.)[9]

Such comic revelations continue without pause. 'The Tell-Tale Heart' is seen to be based upon the primal scene — a witnessing of parental intercourse. Hence it is in the dark that the narrator hears the heart-beat which is like the panting of sexual activity. The old man in the tale is Poe's uncle John Allan who (Bonaparte believes Poe believed) murdered his mother; and so the murderer in the tale punishes the mother's murderer but is also punished himself. (The confessional urge is motivated by two opposite trends: the pressure of conscience, which demands punishment; and instinctual urges towards criminal activities, which may become exhibitionistic.) Though the narrator attributes acuity of vision to the old man's eye, the fact that it is filmed over makes it comparable to a missing eye and, given the assumption that the eye is a substitute for the male genitalia, the old man is castrated. The two contradictory images — that of being acutely sighted and blind (though the blindness is attributed by the analytic interpreter, not by Poe) — condense two successive phases of the criminal father; first, the father castrates the mother to have intercourse with her (it is supposed in psychoanalytic theory that the child believes the mother originally had a penis); and, secondly, he is deprived of his weapon (penis) as punishment.[10]

The variations of interpretation are enormous because priority is not given to the tale but to theoretical associations and patterns which can be variously (because crudely) superimposed upon the tale. It is assumed that the true story will be hidden, that a term can indicate its opposite, or that lack of emphasis upon a given aspect can indicate its significance, and that emotions directed towards one person are directed towards him as a surrogate. Psychoanalytic interpretation involves noting similarities, the two terms of which are then treated as identities, and the significance of the substituted term is explained according to psychoanalytic theory. Such procedures can be both ridiculous and irrefutable because psychoanalytic theory then becomes master, depriving fiction of its highly flexible scope.

Psychoanalytic interpretations (as opposed to psychoanalytic biography) can be roughly divided into three methods, distinguished by degree rather than type. First, there are those that approach the work as a free-for-all allegory, treating each term or image separately, ignoring the work's given structure. This method is akin to dream analysis in which each dream image is considered in isolation and in which the structure of the manifest dream is ignored in favour of the construction of the dream thoughts. Only structures in the manifest dream which might have bearing upon the dream thoughts are noted: sequences in the manifest dream, for example, may represent logical, temporal or causal relationships between the dream thoughts. Secondly, the analytic interpreter may see the art work as a coherent allegory. The structure of the work guides the interpretation. Thus the dramatic events in 'The Pit and the Pendulum' bear at least some similarity to the psychoanalytic drama constructed from it. The man, punished by the Inquisition (i.e., the condemning father) witnesses in the womb prenatal intercourse, and is threatened both by the attacking penis (the pendulum) and the vaginal abyss (the pit). Finally, the psychoanalytic interpreter may choose one dominant image in the work and, having given that a psychoanalytic interpretation, will proceed to explain other images and events in terms of the story indicated by the dominant image. Freud uses this method in his discussion of 'The Sand-Man'.

Though Poe himself loathed allegory and condemned Hawthorne for employing such an indefensible genre, even the free-for-all allegorical approach is acceptable in interpretations of his work simply because the tales are both incomplete and vivid, with a gruesomeness that masquerades as purposive. In some of his tales he does offer psychological explanations of sadism and, not surprisingly, in such cases the psychoanalytic interpreter not merely transforms, but also discards the given material.

In 'The Black Cat' the narrator marries a woman who shares his fondness for animals, and he proceeds to kill his cat and his wife. His behaviour is, he says, a result of perverseness, that is, the impulse of the soul to vex itself, to do wrong simply because it wishes to violate the law. Of course this does not explain anything, but there is sufficient material offered in the tale to use it as a guide to explanation. The narrator reports that from his infancy he was noted for the docility and humanity of his disposition, that indeed his tenderness was such as to make him a jest to his companions. He married early, pleased to find a wife equally docile, sharing his partiality for pets. They also appear to share a sadistic/masochistic partnership: she suffers his drunken rages without complaint and does not resist him when he raises the axe against her, but falls 'dead upon the spot, without a groan'. He kills her because she tries to prevent him killing the cat whose fondness enrages him.

A psychological pattern can be seen within the story. The narrator's docility has made him an object of jest. He prefers domestic animals to people, yet returns their affection with malevolence: he is accustomed to bad treatment; perhaps he has encouraged it; his docility is motivated. When his docility, which is an urge to be denigrated, is met with affection, he not only despises the sources of love and tenderness but must destroy them. This is the most extreme, even egoistic, self-denigration: any being who demonstrates fondness for him deserves to be destroyed.

A psychologically based interpretation, which may well be employed by a psychoanalytic critic, traces patterns in the given material, whereas a strictly psychoanalytic interpretation substitutes one set of terms for another. Thus Bonaparte sees the black cat as Poe's mother. The outline of the cat's body against the burnt dwelling represents both the expression of and punishment for the urethro-phallic eroticism which characterises the small boy's desire for his mother. The fortune lost in the destruction of the narrator's house represents the potency of Poe, which was linked with the loss of his mother. The gouging-out of the cat's eye is, of course, castration, and the hideous wound made by the attack represents the vulva which to some men looks like the wound where castration took place. The narrator buried his wife in an upright position to mock his mother for not having a penis.[11] Thus the patterns genuinely found within the tale are lost.

The more psychological material there is within the story, the more carefully the psychoanalytic critic must proceed, not because the latter is apt to contradict the former but because it then becomes unclear what the psychoanalytic critic is uncovering. Is such a critic analysing the author, or the characters, or a possible patient? Is not the psychoanalytic critic treating the work as though it, or part of it, were material brought forward in analytic sessions? Thus the psychoanalytic critic proceeds as a creator of fictions, interpreting fictions by constructing other fictions of a biographical, historical or clinical nature. Bonaparte's work on Poe is enticing because of the character of Poe's own work, which is both powerful and unsatisfying. Poe's peculiar brand of artistic poverty, linked with his obvious accomplishments, invites another, more controlled story be told alongside his. It makes sense to treat much of his work as though it were material gleaned from analytic sessions, but sense fails when the psychoanalytic critic's fictional assumptions are ignored.

4 The Double: Stevenson's *Dr. Jekyll and Mr Hyde*, Hoffmann's *The Devil's Elixirs*, Dostoevsky's *The Double*

The most common notion of the divided self, or of the double self, is the division between the good and the bad self. This division is remarked upon by Plato in the *Symposium,* and by St. Paul; it is at the root, too, of the plea not to lead us into temptation, for the assumption is that an evil self is ready, given appropriate circumstances, to emerge. R.L. Stevenson's *The Strange Case of Dr Jekyll and Mr Hyde* (1886) makes use of this assumption. A doctor who has had to suppress his more reckless and indulgent impulses on behalf of his career, devises a medicine which, he believes, will release his animalistic nature. The mixture works, and Dr Jekyll becomes Mr Hyde, free to enjoy the pleasures a respected member of society must deny himself: Mr Hyde becomes a front for Dr Jekyll's worse self. The change in character involves such a metamorphosis of appearance that the former cannot be recognised in the latter. Mr Hyde is shorter, and younger than Dr Jekyll, because (Jekyll presumes) Hyde has not lived as long as Jekyll; but these traits also link him to a satyr. Furthermore, in Hyde's appearance there is a deformity that all perceive but none identifies. He bears an aura of distaste and horror, which Jekyll diagnoses as others' unwelcome recognition of affinity.

Jekyll discovers that the creation (or release) of Hyde makes it impossible to keep his unacceptable impulses hidden. He had hoped to save his reputation while lust and anger had a heyday, but he failed to realise that society would not countenance Hyde in any form. Society will execute Hyde, and therefore, to save himself, Hyde must return to the form of Jekyll. But hidden impulses, once released, are out of control. Jekyll spontaneously reverts to Hyde, and the medicine eventually can no longer bring him back to his former self—because, he presumes, the original ingredients contained an unknown impurity which alone was effective.

It is Jekyll's pride, his belief that he can both enjoy and control his impulses, that leads to his destruction. Pentheus, too, in Euripides' *The Bacchae*, is destroyed by Dionysus and his followers because he proudly denies their status. In Hans Werner Henze's '*The Bassarids*' (libretto by Auden and Kallman) the notion of *hubris* is substituted by that of repression: Pentheus is destroyed by the Bacchae because he denies his affinity to them. Jekyll, however, does not deny his own wildness; he tries to find a way to avoid controlling it. Unlike Oscar Wilde's Dorian Gray, Jekyll cannot hide the marks of his crimes away in an attic, for Hyde functions independently, his own proud release mocking Jekyll's proud control.

Poe's 'William Wilson' (1839) divides the good and evil self into two different people who bear the same name, and who, at least in the narrator's mind, have not only disturbingly similar features but also an insidious affinity, so that the narrator's namesake acts as his controlling conscience — a relationship which is uncanny because it is a separate person, not Wilson's own conscience, who interferes with his dishonesty and lechery. Poe's tale is far less satisfactory than Stevenson's. The drama consists of a series of surprises and frustrations, increasing until the narrator finally murders his double. In doing so, he murders all hope of life or Heaven; but there is not, as there is in *The Strange Case of Dr Jekyll and Mr Hyde*, a drama which investigates the need for conscience and for control. As is usually the case with Poe's work, the tale is left to be filled in by the psychoanalytic interpreter. 'William Wilson' can be read as a parable about the id and the super-ego, but it offers no enlightenment on the tension between the two. The fact that it is amenable to such a reading stems from its shallowness, not its profundity.

The double theme is widely discussed in psychoanalytic theory and is explained in various ways. Melanie Klein sees the double as the product of projective identification: a person splits off from himself and ascribes to another those features which he denies as belonging to himself; but because he still unconsciously recognises the projected characteristics as his own, he identifies himself with the other. Thus Klein offers a psychodynamic model in which the mental acrobatics described are doomed to failure, since failure is built into the model: the projected features return home through identification and the attempted denial is ineffective.

Freud's most general analysis of the double theme is closer to the notion of the double as a product of the division between the good and bad self. The ego-ideal, which he eventually reformulated as part of the super-ego, is a psychic structure built up in accord with patterns of authority experienced in the people around the child. At this point Klein's projective identification may be employed to explain the various forms the double may assume: it emerges as the ego aligns itself with the super-ego and projects its worst impulses outwards, in which case the evil tempter is the double of a self that has been denied by this mental mechanism. On the other hand, the ego may align itself with the id, so that the projected figure (as in 'William Wilson') is the super-ego, the figure of conscience and authority.

In his later work Freud emphasised the way in which the super-ego acts as an agent for defence — and it is this function which distinguishes the super-ego from traditional concepts of 'conscience'. The super-ego, Freud believed, arises within the Oedipus complex. The child, in his desire to possess the mother, identifies with the father who actually does possess her. Thus identification serves as a means of overcoming frustration; but, by seeing himself as the father, the child must punish himself in his guise as the child who has erotic desires towards the mother. What began as a defence, then, becomes an attacking, criticising mechanism; but this attacking mechanism is also a defence in that it satisfies the child's guilt feelings for his erotic desires. Here, typically, Freud traces tortuous and devious paths which seem to defeat their own purpose, only to find satisfaction at the last twist in the road.

Identification, which has an important role in analysis of the double, is linked to a range of psychoanalytic suppositions. It is, roughly, the assimilation of one ego to another, as a result of which the first ego behaves like the second in certain respects; the first ego imitates the other and takes it into itself. Thus identification is related to the oral, cannibalistic stage in which love for another person involves the desire to incorporate the other (literally) into one's self; as such, it is the primitive form (part object) of love, preceding love which sees another as an object. When a boy identifies with his father, he wants to be (like) his father; if he makes him the object of his choice, he wants to have him, to possess him.[1] A young man who cannot relinquish his mother for some other sexual object identifies himself with her (thus, defending himself against his inability to possess her, he regresses to the more primitive form of love) and, transformed into her, relinquishing his ego to satisfy his need for her, he looks around for objects to replace his lost ego and upon which he can bestow the love and care his mother lavished upon him. He chooses objects like the young boy his mother loved, and thus becomes a homosexual.[2] Or, as Freud suggested in his essay on Leonardo, the ego, identified with the mother, will choose objects the mother herself would have chosen.[3]

In his study of melancholia Freud also discovered identification at work. The self-reproaches characteristic of the melancholic arise from the fact that the ego has been identified with a lost or relinquished love object (in defence against the loss) and wishes to be revenged upon the lost or abandoned object. Since the self is no longer identified with the ego, the 'self'-reproaches are actually directed towards the lost object.[4] Hysterical symptoms, too, are seen to arise from identification. The sympton shows the point at which the patient has identified with another; the symptom is the other's characteristic acquired by the patient; as a version of synecdoche, it is a means of asserting the identification.

The obvious kinship the double theme has to that of two different personality types within an individual is a result of the fact that the double of one's self implies a tension between the self and the double; the presence of the double challenges the self's existence; it is initially parasitic upon the self, and its aim is to destroy or displace the original self. Otto Rank traces, in psychoanalytic terms, the development of this theme.[5] Originally, in German folklore, the appearance of the double was an omen of death, since it represented one's ghost. Rank believed that this double figure was derived from an earlier, and more comforting, image — that of the soul which survives death. This image stems from narcissism: the libido returns to its initial object — the self and body — when disappointment and frustration are encountered in reality; thus, when faced with the prospect of death, the libido returns to the self, denying the possibility of annihilation. Hostility towards one's double arises from ambivalent feelings towards the self (which, Rank suggests, may be regarded as a defence reaction to narcissism), though the hatred of the double, and its persecutory character, indicate a connection with the sibling complex — the brother presents a rival for the mother's love.

Though the double initially emerged as a protection against extinction of the ego, it is associated with death and therefore represents impending death. It is a theme linked to the frustration of love, or to the destruction of a woman, because narcissism, when seriously threatened (for example, by rejection) becomes more active in compensation, and the double emerges. Freud endorses Rank's analysis: 'This invention of doubling as a preservation against extinction has its counterpart in the language of dreams, which is fond of representing castration by a doubling or multiplication of a genital symbol.'[6] When primary narcissism is superseded, the double takes on its terrifying aspect and proceeds to develop apart from its narcissistic origins. The double represents a splitting-off of the mind's self-criticism so that it shadows its twin and often knows, even without apparent observation, what the original is doing or thinking. Also connected to the double concept, or in some cases represented by the double, are the many possible futures, or selves, to which one clings in fantasy (i.e., desire), 'all the strivings of the ego which adverse external circumstances have crushed, and all our suppressed acts of volition which nourish in us the illusion of Free Will.'[7] The uncanniness of the double theme fits Freud's theory of the uncanny because the double dates back to an early mental stage when it bore an affectionate aspect; but the fact that it has been repressed, and that the double theme re-arouses the discarded fantasy, makes the activation of the theme terrifying.[8]

Schubert's song (poem by Heine) 'Der Doppelgänger' (1828) can be read as a supremely concise realisation of Rank's thesis. The speaker is aghast to see his double standing by the window of his former beloved's house: the chilling and despairing music might be a product of the speaker's annihilation through loss of the love object: he identifies himself with the woman's present lover to mitigate his jealousy, yet the double, originally constructed as a defence, assumes the role of a harbinger of death. Indeed, the speaker's double does foretell his death, or the annihilation of the ego, in so far as it defends against (and thus admits the threat of) such annihilation. However, an interpretation like this, one directed and completed by psychoanalytic theories, is closer to a producer's interpretation of a play or opera which 'realises' the material than to a critic's interpretation which must draw a more definite line between the interesting and the valid. What we are given by the psychoanalyst is one possible framework for the emergence of the song, but this deteriorates to an idiosyncratic supposition when the woman (as she would in Rank's theory) is identified with the mother.

Moreover, the supporting cases should not eclipse counter-examples, and the breadth of possibilities they indicate. Jorge Luis Borges, with characteristic originality, challenges the most fundamental psychoanalytic model of the double theme. He presents self-criticism as a faculty of each half of the double. Each half looks critically and curiously at the other, and each is not one part of a whole but a whole in itself, so that two selves confront each other. In 'Borges and I' from *El Hacedor* the division is roughly between the public and private voice, with the private voice casually objective in its criticism of the other. It is the perfect critical division which Borges underlines, as opposed to the complex and passionate attachment of psychoanalytic divisions within the self. For we are capable of being logical; though this capacity, which might be supposed to lead us away from uncanny effects, leads in Borges's tales directly to the uncanny. 'The Form of the Sword' from *Fictions* startles one not with the gleeful vindictiveness of Moon's narrative of his own cowardice (that he speaks of himself is not disclosed until the end of the tale, and from the surprise this arouses it is clear that there is, ordinarily, a different language used in talking about the self), which Dostoevsky might have attributed to the Irishman (and which would have neatly fitted in to Freud's explanations), but with clear-sighted disdain for his behaviour and motives. In 'The Other' from *The Book of Sand* Borges shows two selves of the same person (divided in this case by time as well as by mutual criticism) failing to acknowledge each other, thus denying the general assumption that the double is peculiarly and deeply attached to its original.

Freud and Rank offer highly interesting formulations of the double, but literary themes range so far from the psychoanalytic explanations, which are themselves loosely thrown together (the narcissistic explanation gives way to an explanation in terms of a self-critical faculty) that the suggestion of analysis, as in the case of Freud's definition of the uncanny, is illusory. What we have from them is provocative handful of double stories to be valued alongside other double tales, not to be seen as explanations of them.

E.T.A. Hoffmann's *The Devil's Elixirs* (1816) is a remarkable and utterly confusing novel in which the double theme is compounded by similar appearance, telepathy, including desire and guilt, and a splitting-up of motive and action between two characters who temporarily fuse and form a single but highly unstable personality. It might be viewed as a Gothic counterpart to *The Comedy of Errors* except that Hoffmann lacks Shakespeare's exuberantly deft manipulation of the material. The proffered explanations with which the novel concludes do not enlighten, but indeed, as Freud says, completely bewilder the reader.[9] Terror and confusion are at the root of the drama, not coincidence and mistakes. *The Devil's Elixirs* might be placed in the picaresque tradition, for the protagonist endures many reversals of fortune, including narrow escapes from punishment and murder, and enjoys easily gained wealth and love; but Hoffmann's novel has none of the light-hearted energy of the picaresque novel, and the protagonist proceeds — or rather is compelled — upon his way not by his wits but by fate's design.

The starting point for the wayward plot is the father's sins which are visited upon his offspring. The protagonist, the Capuchin monk

Medardus, is led from a holy path by lust and pride. He tries to suppress his lust by retreating to a monastery, but he is sent out to the world again, where he commits murder, among other crimes. Finally, he is saved when the woman who has inspired his lust takes holy vows, though she is murdered immediately by Medardus's double. Hoffmann's story belongs to the medieval tradition from which Thomas Mann derived the irony of *The Holy Sinner*. For in spite of Hoffmann's seriousness the repentance he depicts is gròtesque, based upon a sickly, sensuous devotion, and the guilt depicted is hysterical, totally self-regarding, without any glimmer of moral perception.

The Devil's Elixirs does not actually deal with moral transgression, however concerned with it the characters may be. The novel shows the link between the double theme and the demonic, though the demon's horror rests not in his immorality but in his power to confound self-understanding and self-direction. Medardus's life is, from its beginning, spoiled. The theme of the visitation of the father's sins upon the children is Hoffmann's excuse for presenting a person whose thoughts, desires and actions are subject to laws which appear to be far removed from normal human functioning. Medardus's aggression is uncontrolled, not merely in the sense of being unsuppressed, but also in the sense of being undirected — at least by himself. In waking Victor (who, unknown to him, is his brother and his double in appearance) as he lies as the edge of the precipice, Medardus means to save him, yet instead precipitates his fall into the gorge. Here he causes harm without reason and, when he actually does intend to be aggressive to some degree, his aggression is effective in the highest degree. Thus in defending himself against Aurelia's brother, he strangles him. Nor can he protect himself from his own anger, which viciously works against the attainment of his desires. Medardus wants to marry Aurelia — that is the motivation of the main events of his life — and yet he is appalled at the idea of her being his wife. His desire for the woman he idealises becomes a desire to denigrate her, which he will do in marrying her, since in marrying he will break his holy vows, thereby involving her in a sacrilege. Haphazardly, but relentlessly, Hoffmann shows the self nervously jumping away from itself, defeating its own interests and wishes at any given point, but in defiance of any system or rationale.

One could, of course, construct from the story a psychoanalytic hypothesis: Medardus, deprived of his father and believing that his father committed some terrible deed, identifies himself with his father to deny the deprivation and, either to justify his sense of guilt or to exhibit his identification with his father, commits terrible deeds himself. This hypothesis, however, leaves out of account the dynamic self-abuse, terror, love and hatred (in Freud's theory of the melancholic's self-abuse, the abuse is pleasurable, since it is directed not towards the self but towards the person with whom the ego is now identified[10]) that run throughout the novel, and which appear acutely in the following passage. Medardus, posing as a Polish nobleman, but also identified as Count Victor, has just been cleared of murder charges brought against him, for he is now believed not to be Medardus: the mad monk, who is really Count Victor, is now thought to be Medardus. Aurelia has confessed her love to Leonard, as she did earlier to Medardus, and they are about to marry. Medardus narrates the events:

One of the Prince's servants announced that the company was ready to receive us. Aurelia quickly drew on her gloves, and I took her arm. Then the chambermaid suddenly noticed that Aurelia's hair had become disarranged, and hastened away to fetch some hair-pins. The delay seemed to disturb her. As we waited by the door, there was a dull rumbling in the street outside, raucous voices shouted and the noise was heard of a heavy cart, rattling slowly by. I hurried to the window. In front of the palace stood an open cart driven by the hangman's servant. Sitting backwards in it was the monk, in front of whom stood a Capuchin praying aloud with him. The monk was disfigured by a deathly pallor and an unkempt beard, but the features of the gruesome double were only too plain. Crowds were thronging round the cart, and as it moved off he turned his terrible eyes upon me, laughing and howling:

'Bridegroom! Bridegroom! Come on to the roof! Up there we will fight with each other, and the one who pushes the other over will become king, and be able to drink blood!'

'Horrible wretch!' I screamed. 'What do you want with me?'

Aurelia flung her arms round me and tore me away from the window, crying:

'O Holy Virgin! They are leading Medardus, my brother's murderer, to his death! Leonard! Oh, Leonard!'

The demons of hell raged within me, and I seized her in fury.

'Ha, ha, ha! Mad foolish woman! I — I am Medardus! It is I who am your lover, your betrothed — I who am your brother's murderer! You, who are the bride of a monk, will you snivel and whine so that destruction will fall on your bridegroom's head? Ho, ho, ho! I am king and shall drink your blood!'

I let her fall to the floor, drew out my knife and stabbed at her. A fountain of blood gushed over my hand. I rushed down the staircase and fought my way through the crowd to the cart. Seizing the monk, I tore him from his seat. I felt myself gripped from behind, and stabbed about me with my knife. Wrenching myself free, I jumped away but the mob came after me. I felt a wound in my side, but with my knife in my right hand, and dealing powerful blows with my left, I fought my way to the nearby wall of the park and vaulted over it with a tremendous leap.

'Murderer! Murderer! Stop!' shouted voices behind me. I heard them preparing to burst open the gate to the park. I rushed on without stopping. I came to the broad moat which separated the park from the forest until I sank exhausted under a tree.

When I recovered my senses, it was already dark. My only thought was to flee like a hunted beast. I got up but hardly had I moved away when a man sprang out of the bushes and jumped on to my back, clinging to my neck. In vain I tried to shake him off. I threw myself on the ground, jammed my back against the tree, but all to no avail. He cackled and laughed mockingly. Then the moon broke brightly through the black pine-trees, and the pallid, hideous face of the monk, the supposed Medardus, my double, stared at me with glassy eyes as it had done in the cart.

'Hee, hee, hee! Hee, hee, hee! Little Brother! I ... am ... al-ways ... with ... you, will ... not ... leave ... you. Can-not ... run ... like ... you. Must ... must ... carry ... me. Have ... come ... from ... the ... the ... gal-lows. Wanted ... to ... to ... break ... me ... on ... on ... the ... wheel. Hee, hee!'

The horrible spectre laughed and howled. With the strength of wild terror I leapt up like a tiger in the stranglehold of a python, crashing against trees and rocks so as, if not to kill him, at least to wound him so severely that he would be forced to let me go. But he laughed all the more hysterically, and I was the one who received the wounds. I tried to free his hands which were locked under my chin, but he threatened to choke me.

At last, after a fit of frenzy, he suddenly jumped off. I had only to run a few yards when he jumped on me again, cackling and laughing, and stuttering those terrible words. Again that struggle in wild rage — again free — again in the grip of a hideous monster.

I cannot say how long I fled throuh the dark forest, pursued by my double. It seemed an eternity before I ate or drank anything. Of one vivid moment, however, I still have a clear impression: I had just succeeded in throwing him off, when a bright light shone through the forest I heard a monastery bell tolling the matins.

'I have murdered Aurelia!' At this thought the icy arms of death closed around me, and I sank unconscious to the ground.[11]

The references to the Oedipal situation — the challenge of one brother to the other, whereupon one shall drink blood (i.e., spill one's own blood, the blood of the father in castration) and be king (father), the mockery of him as bridegroom before he accepts the challenge — are glaringly obvious because of Freud's persuasive genius, not because of anything we can find in the tale. The disarranged hair here, and elsewhere in the novel, where the arrangement of hair is crucial to Medardus's disguise and to the strange role the barber plays in the events, also stands out like a sore thumb in need of a psychoanalytic bandage; but the obvious madness in the writing, which with its ellipses of motive and meaning, invites psychoanalytic interpretation, provides other more satisfying, even if less complete, indications of meaning.

Medardus has not stabbed Aurelia: even though she was lying prostrate when he attacked her, he did not strike her, but himself. In trying to injure the awful pursuer, he only manages to injure himself. This is a phantom double, a mean, diabolical attacker — no subsequent explanation of Victor's mental state or motive can deny his splendid, fantastical status. Hoffmann shows the double as a thief, as obsession itself is a thief, stealing any possible integration of thought and purpose. The double is the arch-interferer, the arch-reducer, depriving Medardus of all other motives save the compulsion to escape him. The double here is not the bad self versus the good self, but rather an impediment to any self at all. Victor at times enacts Medardus's worst desires, which Medardus himself manages to restrain — Victor stabs Aurelia, who has just taken her vows, at the very moment Medardus has triumphed over the outrage at his loss of the woman — but Victor also at times takes on Medardus's guilt, suffering hysterically from it, and then at other times taunts Medardus as a diabolic conscience. The double here portrays total disintegration.

Despite the flaws of *The Devil's Elixirs,* despite the awkward handling of the religious themes, which really serve only as a background to the horror story, despite the highly unsatisfactory concluding 'explanations' of events, and despite the jolting discontinuity of purpose, *The Devil's Elixirs* has a vigorous and uncanny power, able to suggest issues beyond psychoanalysis. For whatever diagnosis — either of Medardus or Hoffmann — could place the diverse material into a pattern, the novel succeeds in portraying the terrifying instability of the self and the absurd drama of disintegration. This is not merely to say that Hoffmann depicts what it is like to be mad, while psychoanalytic theory describes the mechanisms of madness, for Hoffmann's presentation of the feelings of madness challenges the psychoanalytic model of the double theme in terms of a structured psyche divided within itself; or, rather, Hoffmann reminds us that the structured model itself is a fiction of the same kind as the double story drawn up from volatile and elusive material. *The Devil's Elixirs* defies the assumption, common both to double stories in literature and to double stories in psychoanalytic theory, that the divisions can be identified, that the warring factions have stable aims and comprehensible desires, that indeed the double theme is like a division between two different people. Whereas most double stories indicate the similarities between self-conflicts and interpersonal conflicts, Hoffmann insists upon the differences.

The panicky movement of the plot treads a very delicate balance between mirroring artistically the panic within the self and exhibiting, neurotically, symptoms of such panic. Yet it is fantasy's prerogative to tread this line unsteadily.

Forty years before the publication of *The Strange Case of Dr Jekyll and Mr Hyde* Dostoevsky's *The Double* was published (1846). This is the finest work on the double theme, though, as in *The Devil's Elixirs,* the proliferation of the protagonist's fears becomes a proliferation and fragmentation of themes. Whereas Hoffmann's tale deals with the double's annihilating effect as a breakdown of normal connections between desire and action, intention and effect, even between thought and the thinker, Dostoevsky shows annihilation to be the effect of rejection and redundancy. Golyadkin registers seriously and accurately his colleagues' and acquaintances' attitudes towards him, and his sensitivity to objective self-assessment is disastrous. Medardus on the other hand is merely a subject for confusion. He has little within the normal concept of a self and thus the acts he performs are not clearly assignable to an integrated person or character. Hoffmann's material is nearly impossibly elusive, and though he was able to offer a sketch of original horror, he could not give his fantasy its essential logical or psychological substance.

The Double is sub-titled 'A Poem of St Petersburg', indicating the conditions from which Golyadkin's madness arises. As in any fantasy, the schematic control essential to allegory is ruled out, yet the petty and secular take on a hieratic aspect from Golyadkin's respect which becomes the basis of his defeat.

The story itself is fairly simple. Golyadkin, a Titular Councillor in the

Russian civil service (ranking ninth in a hierarchy of fourteen) attends a party to which he is not invited. After attempting to court the daughter of the house, he is thrown out. On his way home he meets someone who, presumably, is his double. At work the following day he meets the double again. Initially the second Golyadkin is friendly to the first Golyadkin and seems grateful for his help; but gradually the replicated self usurps Golyadkin's work and encourages people to mock him. Golyadkin receives a letter from the young woman he had tried to court, in which she proposes they elope. As he waits for her in the courtyard, he is attacked by a crowd of people and then abducted by his physician (presumably to some prison or madhouse) while the double skips gleefully behind the departing carriage.

Despite the relatively simple narrative it is nearly impossible to give a straightforward account of the story. It is presented from the real Golyadkin's viewpoint who, even at the opening of the tale, is highly disorganised and confused. It seems as though he believes he is invited to the dinner party and at the same time it seems as though he is persona non grata in that house since the servant claims he has orders not to admit him. Furthermore, prior to encountering his double he reports to his physician that enemies are plotting against him. The doctor is subsequently believed to be involved in the plot, for, as Golyadkin recalls the physician's advice to have his medicine dispensed always at the same pharmacy, he implicates the doctor in a plan to poison him. Golyadkin's former landlady, a German woman with whom his replica now lodges, is also perceived as the agent of attacks upon him as punishment for misbehaviour with women.

The fantastic confusion occurs within a pedestrian, realist setting. Golyadkin wakes and wonders whether he is still dreaming. His wakefulness is confirmed by the seediness and tawdriness of his surroundings. As he looks in the mirror the insignificance of his reflection satisfies him:

> 'It would be a fine thing,' said Mr Golyadkin half aloud, 'it would be a fine thing if something was wrong with me today, if a pimple had suddenly appeared out of the blue, for example, or something else disastrous had happened; however, for the moment, it's all right; for the moment everything is going well.'[12]

His first concern is whether his world is the familiar one. His fear is that the common course of petty things will change and take him by surprise. His sense of disaster is as attenuated as his hopes. In comparison, Gregor

Samsa's encounter with the morning's discovery is magnified: Gregor wakes to find himself transformed into a gigantic insect, a metamorphosis consistent with his normal order, whereas a facial pimple constitutes an attack upon Golyadkin whose pathological self-depreciation renders him sufficiently vulnerable to interpret anything as an affront.

Golyadkin's dissatisfaction with his identity — personality, name, position — is the source from which his double arises. Annihilation begins as a defence against self-revulsion. The quandary colloquially expressed as 'not knowing what to do with oneself' can be taken literally in Golyadkin's case. Carefully groomed and riding to the dinner party, he happens to pass in his carriage Andrey Philippovich, his supervisor at work. He wonders, 'Ought I to bow? Should I speak to him or not? Ought I to acknowledge our acquaintance?' and, then,

> Or shall I pretend it's not me but somebody else strikingly like me, and look as if nothing's the matter?' said Mr Golyadkin, lifting his hat to Andrey Philippovich and not taking his eyes off him. 'I . . . It's all right,' he whispered, hardly able to speak, 'It's quite all right; this is not me at all, Andrey Philippovich, it's not me at all, no me, and that's all about it.'[13]

Golyadkin does not value his own actions; he believes that his plans to become socially acceptable are ludicrous. He can admit these desires only by pretending that he is someone else. His belief that people are both right to exclude him and wrong for excluding him exist simultaneously in an imbalance which never leads to self-justification. He protests repeatedly that he is not an intriguer, that he does not wear a mask nor deceive with everyday graces. In reply to this protest his physician suggests that he undergo a radical transformation of character — not an obviously apt reply, but one which shows that even his statements of self-defence appear as self-complaints.

Golyadkin links his inability to wear a mask — that is, to act with composure or even sanity — with the power of his enemies. .He views his disability as a symptom of honesty and forthrightness, but clearly loathes these virtues. He views social composure as self-assertion, and self-assertion as aggression. Thus as Golyadkin frantically endeavours to gain composure in his physician's presence, he sits, then stands, then re-seats himself, and protects

himself against all contingencies with the same challenging stare that possessed such exceptional powers of mentally annihilating and reducing to ashes all enemies of Mr Golyadkin. The stare, moreover, fully conveyed Mr Golyadkin's independence, that is, it stated clearly that Mr Golyadkin didn't care, he was his own master, like anybody else, and his life was his own.[14]

This is precisely what Golyadkin cannot believe. The emergence of his double confirms his worst fears: he is not his own master.

Golyadkin's voluntary actions, or those actions which would normally be considered voluntary, consistently run counter to his decisions. The morning after his initial meeting with his double on the bridge, he determines that he is ill and cannot go to work, but immediately puts on his overcoat and rushes to the office. When Golyadkin does act according to his impulses, those impulses, he believes, mislead him. Thus he reveals to the alternate Golyadkin all his secret hopes about Clara Olsufyevna, whom he had courted at the dinner party. He invites the new Golyadkin to live with him, and no sooner declares that they will be as brothers than he derides himself for his gullibility. On the other hand, if he suppresses his impulses, he also feels that he has made the wrong move. While hiding in the house of Clara Olsufyevna, watching for an opportunity to join the party and approach her, he hesitates and, believing he has missed his chance, he calls himself a coward and a fool, and derides himself not simply for his present behaviour, but for being himself. Yet again, when he behaves bravely, as he believes he does in writing to various people in quest of the new Golyadkin's address, he thinks:

'Why on earth did I write all those letters, like a suicidal idiot? — a suicidal idiot, that's what I am! I couldn't keep my mouth shut, I had to blab. And really, why? If you are ruined, be a doormat. But no, that wouldn't really do for you, you have to bring your pride into it ...'[15]

Thus Golyadkin continually turns against himself; indeed the abuse offers him almost voluptuous satisfaction[16] even as he worries compulsively over others' abuse.

Golyadkin's see-sawing self-image issues in the fear that other people will not know how to distinguish between the two Golyadkins. They will say that one is a rogue and a scoundrel while the other is honest and virtuous, but how will they identify him as the latter and the other Golyadkin as the former? In short, he is uncertain of his status as the object designated by a proper name. His imbalanced view of the qualities of his character issues in confusion as to the identity of his person.

Golyadkin's insecurity arises not from concern with the good and bad self, but from concern with the approved and rejected self. He is obsessed by the notion of shame, and of being sullied. Golyadkin dreams that he is being praised by illustrious company, but suddenly a new figure emerges, the copy of Golyadkin, and shows up the old one as a counterfeit, thus destroying his brief feeling of triumph. Everyone now praises the new Golyadkin and spurns the old. The counterfeit Golyadkin is then multiplied; the city fills with perfect replicas of him. Finally a policeman grabs all the replicas by the collar and locks them up. Golyadkin wakes rigid with horror. He has seen his uselessness, his redundancy; he can be replicated perfectly and without cost. For his interest lies in others' views of him; and therefore whether he is praised or derided, he is inessential, even to himself. His neurosis is the death-throes of self concern. The self must be considered, at least in its own view, as irreplaceable. Freud suggested that the notion of irreplaceability, when it is active in the unconscious, may appear as an endless series since every surrogate is inadequate,[17] yet Dostoevsky's tale suggests the horror of discovering that something believed to be irreplaceable is in fact easily replaceable. The horror arises from the inability to sustain self-valuation which indeed often does seem to defy a realistic assessment of the self and which at the same time is so necessary to human functioning that it must also been seen as realistic. Dostoevsky brings objectivity into the self and in so doing challenges the feasibility of self-knowledge.

Golyadkin is anxious to have the whole affair settled and he believes, or seems to believe, he has a good idea of what the affair is about, though the reader does not. He believes that the case has actually been settled against him, and that all he has to do is to surrender to the enemy; then he could give up the struggle, then he could rest. As soon as he sees the double he believes that the verdict is signed and sealed; he tries to feel relieved, tries to feel that it does not matter to him (for, when he is acutely embarrassed or frightened, he pretends that it all has nothing to do with him, that he is someone else), yet he cannot suppress dread:

> [. . .] suddenly his whole body quivered, and involuntarily he leapt to one side. He began to look around him with inexplicable anxiety; but there was nobody, nothing particular had happened, and yet . . . and yet it seemed to him that just now, this very moment, somebody had been standing there, close to him, by his side, also leaning on the parapet and — an extraordinary thing! — had even said something to him, something hurried and abrupt, not altogether understandable, but about a matter touching him very nearly, something that

concerned him [...] Mr Golyadkin was troubled and even afraid, and felt at a loss. It was not that he feared this might be some bad character, he was simply afraid [...] The fact was that the unknown now seemed to him to be somehow familiar [...] Mr Golyadkin knew this man thoroughly well; he even knew what he was called, knew his name [...] His situation at that moment was like that of a man standing above a terrible chasm when the ground has begun to break away [...] Mr Golyadkin knew and felt, was indeed quite sure, that some other evil thing would inevitably happen to him on the way, something else unpleasant would burst upon him; for instance, he might meet the stranger again; but, horrible to tell, he even wanted the meeting, felt it was unavoidable and only asked for the whole thing to be over and done with as quickly as possible ... [18]

Golyadkin chases his double back to his own flat where he finds the 'stranger' sitting on his bed, greeting him with a friendly nod; he does not want to flee his replacement.

Clearly Golyadkin's anxiety is not rational; that is, it does not arise from an external danger ('It was not that he feared this might be some bad character, he was simply afraid [...]') but from something that can be effected within himself. To speak of his anxiety in psychoanalytic terms as fear arising from an internal danger, however, is to neglect the logic of his thoughts and the way they register his external reality.

The following morning he acknowledges that for a long time something was being prepared, that 'there was *somebody else* in reserve.' In effect, given his objective value, there is always someone else in reserve; Golyadkin as Titular Councillor is easily replaceable, and he lacks either genuine attachments or necessary fantasies of self-importance as protection against this recognition. His acute sensitivity to impersonal forces leads him to suspect that they are directed against him in particular, and he thereby imparts to them personal features. He scans these features for confirmation of self-importance, or of the significance of his uniqueness, yet the impersonal cannot provide this confirmation. Dissatisfied, he avidly repeats his search for recognition, and repeated frustrations defeat him. Thus it is his dependence upon others' responses, alongside the recalcitrant impersonality of those responses, that annihilate him — or, rather, effect the annihilation of which such obssessive concern itself is a symptom.

The mockery Golyadkin endures as a result of his dependence is both cheap and violent. He continually broods upon the idea of having his reputation sullied; his concern with dirt can be taken literally. The stairs to his flat are filled with rubbish. When he first chases the double to the flat he is surprised that the 'stranger' knows his way about these dirty obstacles. When Golyadkin gets soiled walking along the street, he believes that it is all part of the plot against him. He associates himself with dirt, and when he sits at a restaurant table and notices a pile of dirty dishes at his table, he believes he is responsible for them, though everyone laughs at him when he asks how much he owes for the meal. (The rationale of this query is in past experience: his double takes meals at restaurants and then disappears, so that Golyadkin is deemed accountable for the bill. The double is, moreover, surprisingly greedy. While he has one patty, his double has ten so that Golyadkin has the responsibility for eleven.) The most humiliating moment occurs when his double greets their colleagues with the confident geniality of a popular man. Eagerly Golyadkin junior takes the hand of Golyadkin who responds with tearful emotion; but, suddenly, when the new Golyadkin realises whose hand he is clasping, he pulls, back, shaking his hand as though to rid himself of the attachment to filth.

In the wake of this humiliation the new Golyadkin teases the old about his association with women: 'Give me a kiss, darling!' he calls out, and everyone present enjoys the sly allusion. Clearly Golyadkin's defeat has some link to his relations with women. His initial self-inflicted humiliation occurs as he forces his attention upon Clare Olsufyevna, and his final defeat occurs as he waits for her in the courtyard in compliance with either a terrible prank or the message in a hallucinated letter which suggests that they elope. The 'letter' generates Golyadkin's most disagreeable thoughts. Angry at her suggestion, he considers that it proves how badly she, and indeed all women, are reared, expecting men to make love all the time, when, in fact, all a man really wants is someone to cook and clean and to be satisfied with an occasional little kiss. Previously he has suspected his former landlady, a one-eyed German woman, of leading the plot against him and of spreading the rumours which incite an acquaintance to accuse him of being dangerous to morally innocent and uncontaminated people; but now he sees the ex-landlady as the good woman and Clara Olsufyevna as the bad witch. Yet he waits for her in the courtyard, as the letter bids him. He waits for her, feeling only anger towards her: 'Here's a man on his way to destruction, a man losing his identity, and he can hardly control himself — and you talk about a wedding!'[19]

Golyadkin does not have to repeat the assertion that he would cut off his finger to effect an instantaneous settlement, to involve the psychoanalytic theme of castration complex. Golyadkin looks upon his superiors as paternal figures — if he can win them over to his side, they will save him; but the new Golyadkin wins them for himself, and thereby renders the old Golyadkin helpless. He is even attacked for his desire for women, which he simultaneously repudiates and pursues, waiting in the courtyard to elope and deriding the notion of romantic attachment. While vainly expecting satisfaction, he is carried off by the physician, another paternal figure, as his double stands mocking him from behind. The double may be the just punisher of his desires, as well as the idealised other who succeeds where Golyadkin himself fails. The one-eyed landlady could bear her deformity as a sign that she is the avenging (i.e. castrating) woman, and therefore Golyadkin, in preparing to satisfy his desire with Clara Olsufyevna, thinks of her as the good woman (for she punishes forbidden desires) and Clara Olsufyevna as the bad woman (for she grants the satisfaction of forbidden desires).

Though one cannot legitimately argue against psychoanalytic interpretation in general by postulating one interpretation and showing it to be inadequate, since psychoanalytic theory does permit an enormous range of critical interpretation, it can be said that any such interpretation is in many respects closer to the crative realisation of the producer of a play or opera than the explication, emphases and registers of response attempted by the literary critic. The producer is free to distort so long as his distortions are enlightening, but critical re-writings tend to be far less interesting. Fiction does not lend itself as easily to creative realisation since it is not something to be performed. Moreover, in good fiction, the detail, the structure, the allusions offered within the work itself are usually too dense to be amenable to idiosyncratic translations. The castration theme may well be indicated in Dostoevsky's *The Double,* but in making use of this indication the story's strength must be seen as equal to that of the psychoanalytic theory, whereby the castration theme becomes enmeshed in more general problems of the self.

The double fantasy makes use of the fact that, when notions of the mind and self are involved, the metaphor becomes the only possible method of presentation. The double fantasy exploits the fact that the language of actuality is usually logically prior to metaphorical language: we must know what a red rose newly sprung in June is before we can understand how love is like it, and we must see a person against another identical person to understand what a conflict within the self is like. The double theme has therefore been exploited as a means of presenting as actual that which can only be presented in metaphor, and the exploitation has had such success because self-conflicts are felt as actual conflicts between separate but affinitive forces. For this reason, too, psychoanalysis has had such success: it presents fundamentally metaphorical material in the guise of historical explanation, and it can evade detection because its metaphors are peculiarly intricate and systematic, and because (given the material it deals with) it can be countered only by another metaphor. The supposition that psychoanalytic theory alone is not metaphorical but literal, is, as I shall show in the final chapter, highly misleading.

5 Fantastic Objectivity: Franz Kafka

The writers discussed thus far have been forced into the realm of fantasy by the collapse of objectivity. Ordinarily perceptions provide information about the external world; there is usually sufficient agreement about that world to postulate objectivity. The fantasist presents conditions in which ordinary anticipation is in abeyance, not because perceptions fail to supply data but because there is no method for distinguishing perceptions which register common agreement from those which register an idiosyncratic and possibly insane vision.

I now consider the fantasists who accept the absence of normal expectations and agreements as though they had never existed. The course of events may give rise to pain and despair, but not surprise, since there is no norm from which deviation would legitimately justify surprise. Their task is to create the conditions and laws of a new reality in which even achievement brings despair since their new logic is constructed precisely upon the defeats and deficits of our readily recognisable world.

By comparing the *Michael Kohlhaas* of Heinrich Kleist (whom Kafka greatly admired) with Kafka's own work, we can see how the later writer transforms 'objective' or rational protests and their associated confusions into superficially neurotic concerns which highlight actual conditions. *Michael Kohlhaas* (1811) is based on the case of Hans Kohlhaas, and gives an account of sixteenth-century horse dealer who, in travelling to Dresden, is detained by Junker Wenzel von Tronka. The Junker claims Kohlhaas's horses as payment for traversing his land. The outraged Kohlhaas dedicates himself to the redressment of this wrong. But his determination to obtain justice sets all possible balance awry. To meet legal costs he mortgages his home. To avenge himself he storms the Junker's castle and attacks Wittenberg, and then Leipzig, in the mistaken belief that the Junker is there. Kohlhaas tries to present a petition to the Elector of Saxony but it is quashed by the Elector's corrupt courtiers.

Moreover, Kohlhaas's wife dies from an injury inflicted upon her by one of the courtiers as she tries to deliver her husband's petition to the Elector. Eventually Kohlhaas agrees to settle the matter if he is compensated for his horses, but the von Tronka family delay payment. Since Kohlhaas's dispersed followers are raiding the country under a different leader, but in his name, Kohlhaas is imprisoned. The present leader of his band writes to Kohlhaas offering to engineer his escape, but the letter is intercepted, and Kohlhaas is discredited when his acceptance of the offer is published. Even though the Elector of Brandenburg learns of the matter and dismisses the official who brought about Kohlhaas's disgrace, he insists, for political reasons, that Kohlhaas be tried by a Berlin court. The Elector of Saxony offers to have him reprieved in exchange for an important secret, but Kohlhaas rejects his bargain and is beheaded. Nevertheless, prior to his execution his horses, restored to their former good condition, are returned to him. Moreover, the Junker is sentenced. Thus is justice done.

Michael Kohlhaas shares K.'s and Joseph K.'s belief that law will, ultimately, ensure justice, and that a meeting with a supreme law official will save him. Michael Kohlhaas's need to clarify his position, like that of K., dissipates his life. He virtually worships those who might offer him justice, though Kleist depicts the officials' motives as personal and petty, having little relation to justice. Nevertheless, Michael Kohlhaas employs the oridinary concept 'justice': the Junker has stolen and mistreated his horses; therefore the Junker should be punished and Kohlhaas compensated. He may indeed be mad to invest so much to settle the matter, but his reasoning fits an ordinary conceptual framework.

In Kafka's works, however, the initial crime or unjust act is replaced and obliterated by accusation and guilt: what is in ordinary logic a necessary precedent is now ignored, and a new logic of guilt is explored. *The Trial* (1925) opens with the arrest of Joseph K. for an unstated crime and proceeds to describe Joseph K.'s anxious and confused attempts to obtain a proper hearing, and then the helplessness at his trial which leads to his degrading execution; but Kafka's shorter works present the crucial themes with greater power and precision. In the parable 'Before the Law' (1919; also used as part of *The Trial*) a man seeking admittance to the law is told by the door-keeper that he cannot enter immediately. As he waits he looks at the open door. Suspecting that he is hoping to sneak past, the door-keeper laughs and tells the man that even if he were to get past this first entrance, he would be stopped by other door-keepers. The man waits for years. He grows old and his eye-sight fails, but in the darkness he can distinguish a radiance issuing from the gateway. He asks the door-keeper why, since everyone seeks understanding of the law, no one else has come this way. The door-keeper answers: 'No one else could ever be admitted here, since this gate was made only for you. I am now going to shut it.'[1]

This tale is called a parable, but the lessons it contains are facts rather than precepts: our lives will be wasted by futile hopes and efforts; not only do our own goals set traps for us, but some obscure power seems intent upon reinforcing and misdirecting those aims; we will be fooled and mocked.

The futility of 'worthy' pursuits is linked in Kafka's work with arbitrary or idiosyncratic accusation, for paths are blocked as punishment, or, more precisely, our aims are diverted by guilt, and we become self-defeating in consequence of that guilt. 'The Judgement' highlights the cruelly arbitrary nature of accusation alongside its compelling and irrational powers. At the opening of the tale George Bandemann sits in his room, reflecting upon what advice to give a friend who emigrated to Russia. At first the friend was successful in his new home, but his business is now failing, as is his health, and he is lonely. George wonders whether to tell his friend of his own forthcoming marriage, and considers how to placate the envy such news is sure to evoke. After reflection, George sends his friend an invitation to the wedding and then enters his father's room, where his previous complacency dissolves. As he assumes the role of the reassurer — telling his father that he is still necessary to the success of the family business, that his own friends will never take the place of his father — and then the role of protector — trying to persuade his father to lie down, even lifting him from his chair and helping him off with his dressing gown — he suddenly thinks, 'My father is still a giant of a man.' As he puts his father to bed the old man asks whether he is well covered-up, and then adds, 'You want to cover me up, I know, my young sprig, but I'm far from being covered up yet.'[2]

The father's confrontation of his son's covert desires is accompanied (and made plausible) by spiralling praises of the emigrated friend which conclude with the assertion that the man in St Petersburg would have been — unlike George — a son after his own heart. Thus it seems that George's anticipation of his friend's envy at the news of his forthcoming marriage was an expression of his own envy; it had been necessary to depreciate his friend with pity before he could communicate his own plan to marry. The father's dissatisfaction with his son becomes devastation through mockery — in particular, a mockery of George's desire to marry, ending with condemnation of his entire life:

'Because she lifted up her skirts,' his father began to flute, 'because she lifted her skirts like this, the nasty creature,' and mimicking her he lifted his shirt so high that one could see the scar on his thigh from his war wound, 'because she lifted her skirts like this and this you made up to her, and in order to make free with her undisturbed you have disgraced your mother's memory, betrayed your friend and stuck your father into bed so that he can't move. But he can move, or can't he?'

And he stood up quite unsupported and kicked his legs out. His insight made him radiant.

George shrank into a corner, as far away from his father as possible. A long time ago he had firmly made up his mind to watch closely every least movement so that he should not be surprised by any indirect attack, a pounce from behind or above. At this moment he recalled this long-forgotten resolve and forgot it again, like a man drawing a short thread through the eye of a needle.

'But your friend hasn't been betrayed after all!' cried his father, emphasizing the point with stabs of his forefinger. 'I've been representing him here on the spot.'

'You comedian!' George could not resist the retort, realized at once the harm done and, his eyes starting in his head, bit his tongue back, only too late, till the pain made his knees give.

'Yes, of course I've been playing a comedy! A comedy! That's a good expression! What other comfort was left to a poor old widower? [...] And my son strutting through the world, finishing off deals that I had prepared for him, bursting with triumphant glee and stalking away from his father with the closed face of a respectable business-man! Do you think I couldn't have loved you, I, whom you turned your back on?'

Now he'll lean forward, thought George; what if he topples and smashes himself! These words went hissing through his mind.

His father leaned forward but did not topple. Since George did not come any nearer, as he had expected, he straightened himself again.

'Stay where you are, I don't need you! ... I am still much the stronger of us two. All by myself I might have had to give way, but your mother has given me so much of her strength that I've established a fine connection with your friend and I have your customers here in my pocket!'

'He has pockets even in his shirt!' said George to himself, and believed that with this remark he could make him an impossible figure for all the world. Only for a moment did he think so, since he kept forgetting everything.

... 'How long a time you've taken to grow up! Your mother had to die, she couldn't see the happy day, your friend is going to pieces in Russia, even three years ago he was yellow enough to be thrown away, and as for me, you see what condition I'm in. You have eyes in your head for that!'

'So you've been lying in wait for me!' cried George.

His father said pityingly, in an off-hand manner: 'I suppose you wanted to say that sooner. But now it doesn't matter.' And in a louder voice: 'So now you know what else there is in the world besides yourself, till now you've known only about yourself! An innocent child, yes, that you were, truly, but still more truly have you been a devilish human being. And therefore take note; I sentence you now to death by drowning!'

George felt himself urged from the room, the crash with which his father fell on the bed behind him was still in his ears as he fled [...] Out the front door he rushed, across the roadway, driven towards the water. Already he was grasping at the railings as a starving man clutches food. He swung himself over, like the distinguished gymnast he had once been in his youth, to his parents' pride. With weakening grip he was still holding on when he spied between the railings a motor-bus coming which would easily cover the noise of his fall, called in a low voice: 'Dear parents, I have always loved you, all the same,' and let himself drop.[3]

Freud's influence, and his greatness, are such that it is impossible not to see his Oedipal theory at work here (though one should not suppose that a 'Freudian' interpretation reveals what Freud would have said): the scar high up on the father's leg might indicate (attempted) castration, as would the son's protectiveness, which the father views as an attack; the father remains the stronger of the two because he has the mother's support — that is, he maintains his possession of her; the son tries to belittle the father but cannot concentrate on this task, whereas the father succeeds briliantly. The friend is the good son, who leaves the home rather than attack the father to gain possession of the mother, though his goodness makes him impotent ('even three years ago he was yellow enough to be thrown away'). George is the innocent child, but also the devilish human being because, as a child, he desires his mother and longs to castrate the father — a devilish thing to do. His (bad) father sentences him to death by drowning — that is, he must return to the womb. The man rushing to fulfil this sentence is also the boy fleeing the primal scene ('the crash with which his father fell on the bed behind him was still in his ears as he fled'). The punishment both achieves his aim (admittance to the womb, with his entire body representing his genitals) and satisfies his guilt. At the same time he confirms his love for his parents, which is reciprocated even by his vengeful father ('Do you think I couldn't have loved you, I, whom you turned your back on?')

A psychoanalytic interpretation of 'The Judgement' offers superficial satisfaction in that it brings the puzzling narrative under control, but it ignores the obvious emphasis within the tale — George's humiliation as he compares himself with his father. The explanation for this humiliation is not derived from the castration theme, but from the delicate relation of the self to certain types of comparison and criticism: Kafka describes the self giving way beneath the father's pronouncements when the latter assumes the role of judge. The notion of the father as judge is so terrifying, so *unjust,* that it presents the father with a recalcitrantly cruel face. The child is both innocent and devilish for a myriad of reasons (any desire to possess the mother and castrate the father should be seen within a mass of impulses and, along with many other impulses, half-formed, not fully motivating), and a severe sentence might be warranted if the father were a judge and if the child's inchoate impulses and aims were to be viewed in terms of innocence or guilt. In such a case, 'justice' would be both absurd and terrifying.

Freud saw the super-ego as the legacy of the Oedipal phase, and the authoritarian character of the super-ego not as a realistic representation of the parental figures but as wearing rather more severe and threatening features. As such, a psychoanalytic explanation of 'The Judgement' would account for the excessive anger and vengefulness of George's father in terms of George's guilt-feelings and fears; but the astonishing clarity of Kafka's fantasy points to the reality of those fears. In 'The Judgement' George suffers not from his own fears projected on to his father but from his sensitivity to what his father is actually doing to him. He *is* drowned by the power of his father's personality. Marriage is impossible because his father's distrust and mockery defeat the integration of purpose and responsibility. He discovers envy, and its accompanying humiliations, at the root of every attachment, however much reason he may have for contentment. The father's attack, with its transformations and contradictions, forms a fantastic picture, but also a highly accurate picture of what a father does to his son by means of certainty, severity, mockery and egoism.

Any action can be described in a number of ways, and the intention of the actor, whether conscious or unconscious, is not always relevant to a description of the action. Kafka re-describes unintentional actions and consequences as though they were intentional, thus uncovering the insult within the injury. He implies, 'If you had wanted to do this, you could not have done a better job.' Then the logic of intentional harm takes over, and its consequences are not merely contemplated but also experienced. The father is blamed not only for his actions but also for all possible effects of possible actions. The exaggeration also, however, depicts the effects as they are felt: George's impasse is that he cannot marry, cannot maintain self-respect and self-direction and self-responsibility; he feels himself to be drowned. The tale dramatises realistic responses.

(Lacan says that transference is the acting-out of the reality of the unconscious and, previously, I.A. Richards had noted that transference was a form of metaphor: one thing or person is treated as though it were another. Thus the writing of the story itself, the 'translation' of mental phenomena into a drama, might be viewed as a psychoanalytic mechanism.[4] This view would take nothing away from the story, if it were acknowledged (as it would be by Lacan but not by Freud) that the reality presented by the story cannot, if the story is a good one, be better supplied, or finally supplied, by psychoanalysis with a master-story.) George's immediate recognition of his guilt is based not upon forbidden desires and fears of punishment, as it would be if it fitted into the Oedpal theme, but upon self-disappointment confirmed by his father's disappointment. Guilt, as Kafka makes obvious, is experienced in consequence not only of actions or desires thought to be immoral, but also of any failure to attain an ideal. Responsibility, as I shall show in subsequent discussions of Kafka's work, is shifted from its usual centrality in the concept of guilt and in its place is a depressive, unstable and terrified view of the self as a potential actor caught up in others' demands and expectations.

The Oedipus complex falls within the usual sequence of transgression, guilt and punishment. To see Kafka's work in this context is to limit its importance and bring it back within the scope of Kleist's tale.

Comparison with Chekhov's 'Ward Six' (1892), which deals, as do *The Trial* and *The Castle,* with fear of committing a crime adventitiously and of subsequent prosecution, will serve to bring out Kafka's original use of fantasy, which legitimately resists psychoanalytic explanation. Gromov's condition bears marked similarity to that of Joseph K.:

He knew he was not guilty of any crime, and was quite confident he would never commit murder or arson, or steal; but then it was not so difficult to commit a crime by accident, without meaning to. And is there not such a thing as wrongful accusation or miscarriage of justice?

... And in the present state of the law, a miscarriage of justice is more than likely and there is nothing unusual about it [. . .]

Next morning Gromov got out of bed in a state of terror and with cold sweat on his forehead. He was absolutely certain that he might be arrested any minute. The fact that the painful thoughts of the previous day would not leave him, he concluded, must mean that there was a grain of truth in them. After all, they could not have entered his head without some reason.

[. . .] Gromov spent the days and nights that followed in a state of anguish. He thought the people who passed his windows or entered his yard were spies or detectives [. . .] He began to keep to himself and shun people. His job, which he had always detested, now became intolerable to him. He was afraid of a frame-up, of someone slipping some money in his pocket without his being aware of it and then accusing him of taking bribes; or that he would himself unwittingly make some mistake in an official document, which would be tantamount to forgery; or that he would lose money that did not belong to him.[5]

In *The Interpretation of Dreams* Freud discusses a relevant case. An obsessional neurotic is afraid he is going to kill someone. He supposes, whenever he learns that a murder has been committed, that he will be accused. As a consequence, he is always manufacturing alibis. Eventually he finds it impossible to leave home, lest he actually kill. Freud's analysis explains that the man, after his father's demise, is haunted by his death wishes towards the father. The rationale behind his phobic symptoms is: anyone wishing to kill his father cannot be trusted to spare the lives of people less closely related to him; he should therefore be locked in his room as a potential criminal.[6]

This analysis might well be applicable to Gromov's case without distorting the point and purpose of Chekhov's tale, but such analyses impede and even falsify the reading of Kafka's work, for they presuppose an idiosyncratic context which deviates from a rational framework of motive, action and aim, but which is restored within that framework through the elucidation of unconscious motives and feelings. Kafka, however, presents apparent abnormality to re-define the normal. K.'s 'neurotic' timidity registers the nature of authority; if it does register his (or the author's) unconscious motives, then it does so only incidentally. Like Kleist, Kafka presents in *The Castle* an authority who acts meanly and selfishly and who is protected by corrupt officials, but whereas Kleist shows the law being misused, neglected or distorted, Kafka demonstrates the disintegration of the concept of 'law' with only personal whim and self-interest at stake, so that compliance means obeying the law-giver's pleasure. In this way he accentuates the despair within our need to please and links it to respect for authority (both the authority of the law, which is related to guilt, and the authority of society, which is related to acceptance and affection) which, Kafka shows, can be conceptually distinguished from respect for what the authority represents. Certainly K. does respect both Klamm and the rules of the Castle, but in fact the Castle's bureaucrat does not represent rules or laws, only arbitrary preferences backed by an unreflecting objective justification of those preferences. As in 'The Judgement' guilt is tied to the failure to please. Kafka's 'distortions' offer a new moral language, purely psychological, where guilt arises from what one is, rather than from what one does or has done. Consequently morality becomes a nightmare. There is no place in 'The Judgement' or *The Trial* for the disintegration of moral principles that occurs in 'Heart of Darkness'. Moral concepts are fragmented from the beginning, and for this reason the characters are haunted by enigmatic punishments and indecipherable sins.

Nathaniel Hawthorne, who generally had a firm conceptual grasp of sin, does, in one of the *Twice Told Tales,* share Kafka's sensitivity to a force both avenging and outside the normal framework of morality. Moreover, Hawthorne presents this force not with Jehovah's grandeur but with the features of the petty, idiosyncratic judge familiar in Kafka's works. 'Wakefield' (1835) is the story of a man who has been married for ten years and is fond of hoarding little secrets from his wife. Bidding her good-bye, casting her a mysterious smile, he says he will return in a few days. He takes lodgings near his home and spies on his wife to see how she conducts herself in his absence. He believes that he will soon return home, but he is always tempted to wait a little longer. Ten years pass. Their eyes meet as she, dressed as a widow, passes him on the way to church; but she does not recognise him. Ten more years pass. He creeps up to the house where he sees his wife's profile reflected by the firelight upon the wall. He suddenly enters the house, greeting her with the same mysterious smile he cast in parting, and re-assumes his former domesticity.

'Wakefield' is in some respects a parabolic re-writing of the Rip Van Winkle story, and Hawthorne certainly does not cease to draw moral lessons from Wakefield's behaviour: 'The vagueness of the project, and the convulsive effort with which he plunges into the execution of it, are equally characteristic of a feeble-minded man,' Hawthorne comments, and when Wakefield is intrigued to learn the effect his absence will have the author concludes, 'A morbid vanity, therefore, lies nearest the bottom of the affair.' As habit guides Wakefield to his own front door, from which he turns away in fear, Hawthorne writes, 'At that instant his fate was turning on the pivot. Little dreaming of the doom to which his first backward step devotes him, he hurries away.'[7] Thus Wakefield obliterates the possibility of choice and behaves as one dead, forfeiting the living person's influence upon human interests and sympathy. Yet Hawthorne's clear-eyed judgements ignore the story he tells. For Wakefield cannot be held up as an example of vanity's revenge or pride's downfall or the consequences of weak will. He exhibits, but does not suffer from life-arrest. He is pathetic because his wasted life does not matter, and his self-inflicted 'punishment' is really the abject acceptance of his own unimportance. The enormous respect with which Hawthorne treats the story transforms the ridiculous into the criminal, and, as in Kafka's world, the onus of guilt is borne by the person as an individual, on account of his preferences and whims which, ordinarily, would not be considered in a moral light. Wakefield's guilt is that of George Bandemann's and Gregor Samsa's; it is the inability to escape insignificance.

The transformation theme is utilised in modern fantasy to indicate, as does the double theme, doubts about our own identity, about that of others, and about the way in which our relations with others affect our identity. The modern use is linked to its mythic counterpart in which metamorphosis provides special powers of disguise and, frequently, of mobility; but in modern fantasy these concomitant powers turn against the protagonist, preying upon guilt and impotence. The powers that were once divine are magnified by their pedestrian settings in a way that dramatises, not waylays, ignorance and fear.

In the opening of Philip Roth's novel *Portnoy's Complaint* (1969) the patient-narrator reports his childhood belief that his mother was everywhere, that she existed in every woman: he sees her in his schoolteacher and runs home, hoping to beat her, or to catch her in the act of transformation, but he finds her already there, composed and cheerful, secure in her new self. This promising fantasy, however, is not developed. Portnoy presents it to his analyst, and Roth himself does not put it to use. Gogol, in contrast, develops a similar fantasy as the means by which certain fears are dramatised and explored. 'Ivan Fyodorovich Shponka and His Aunt' (1831) is a tale about a modest, obedient lieutenant who resigns his post when his aunt asks him to help her run his estate, which she has managed herself for several years. When he arrives, he is surprised by her vigour and health, for her excuse in calling him back is that she is growing old. It soon becomes clear that she is determined to see him married, and with this realisation the unremarkable young man develops a profoundly terrible and comic imagination:

But Ivan Fyodorovich stood there thunderstruck. True, Marya Griogoryevna was quite pretty; but to get *married*! The idea seemed so inconceivable, so far from his world, that he just could not think about it without a profound feeling of terror. Live with a *wife*! It was just unheard of! He would never be alone in his room anymore, because there would always be *two* of them, together, everywhere! The sweat poured off his face the more engrossed he became in these thoughts. He went to bed earlier than usual, but, however hard he tried, he just could not drop off.

In the end long-awaited sleep, that universal comforter, descended on him. But what dreams he had! He had never known such chaotic nightmares before. First he dreamt that everything around him was making a terrific din and whirling round and he was running, running, without feeling the ground under his feet, until he could run no longer. Suddenly someone grabbed him by the ear. 'Ah, who's that?' 'It's me, your wife!' a voice shouted right into his ear. And he suddenly woke up. Then he had another dream, that he was already married, that everything in the house had become very strange and peculiar, and that there was a *double* instead of single bed in his room. His wife was sitting on a chair. He was completely at a loss what to do, whether to go up to her or speak to her, and then he noticed she had the face of a goose. He looked the other way, and saw another wife, and she had a goose's face as well. He looked again and there was a third wife; he looked around — still another. He panicked and ran into the garden, but it was hot out there. He took off his hat — and there was a wife sitting in it. Beads of sweat trickled down his face. He felt in his pocket for his handkerchief — and found a wife in it. He took some cotton wool out of his ear — there was a wife there too. Suddenly he started jumping around, and Auntie looked at him and said in a serious voice: 'Yes, you may well jump around, because you're a married man now.' He went over to her, but Auntie had turned into a belfry and someone was hauling him up by a rope to the top. 'Who's pulling me up?' he asked in a pathetic voice. 'It's me, your wife, and I'm hauling you up because you're a bell.' 'No, I'm not a bell, I'm Ivan Fyodorovich!' he shouted. 'No, you're a bell,' said a certain colonel of the P— infantry regiment who happened to be passing at the time. Then he had another dream, that his wife was not

a person at all, but some kind of woollen material. He had gone into a
shop in Mogilev. 'What kind of material would you like, sir?' asked
the shopkeeper. 'Have some *wife,* it's the latest thing now! Lovely
quality as well. Everyone's having coats made from it.' The
shopkeeper made his measurements and cut the wife up. Ivan
Fyodorovich took it under his arm and went off to a Jewish tailor,
who said, 'No, that's *very poor* material. No one uses *that* kind of stuff
for coats now [. . .]' Ivan Fyodorovich woke up terrified, with cold
sweat pouring off him.[8]

Gogol's tale concludes on this horrible note. The abrupt end, after this
brief black flowering of Ivan Fyodorovich's imagination is disappointing,
but the impact of the dream is such that one can see that it has no end.
Ivan Fyodorovich exhibits neurotic anxiety which is as amenable as
Portnoy's to psychoanalysis; for though there is no reason to suppose his
obvious sexual quandary is unconscious, it could be seen in the context of
unconscious fears and identifications. Yet whatever idiosyncrases are thereby revealed the arresting power of this fantasy is in its ability to fragment
the ordinary concept of marriage and to penetrate the ordinary fragments
with unusual horror. This is what it is to be married, Ivan Fyodorovich
realises. Sharing a home with a wife is as he imagines: everywhere he
turns, he will see her, or see evidence of her (in his hat, his pocket, his
handkerchief). She will be as close to him as his clothes, but unlike them,
he will not be able to cast her off. It is his protest against her presence that
makes any reminder of her a complete representation of her. His aunt, the
belfry, he, the bell, and his wife, the rope-puller tell how the aunt
encapsulates him, while he must remain passive to the attack of the
ringing bell: he not only gives up his identity in marrying but also loses
control of his modest pace of life. Ivan Fyodorovich does not uncover new
aspects of marriage, but reveals a grotesque quality of familiar aspects. His
dream is a perfectly accurate scenario of marriage without the desire to be
married, his resistance to marriage can be seen as a perfectly rational
position.

   The one element in Ivan Fyodorovich's dream which would be helped
by psychoanalytic interpretation is the role of Auntie herself, who instigates
and dominates his fear. Why, for example, is her desire to see him
married so threatening? Why, that is, does her desire make him live
through all the awfulness of marriage, as though her desire had immediate
effect? It is the aunt who confirms for him that it is necessary to be
submissive now that he is married, and it is the aunt as the belfry who
envelops the helpless bell. The aunt's function in the tale is to precipitate

her nephew's fears, but it is unclear why she is able to fulfil her function so effectively, and a supplementary, psychoanalytic, story, would have interest here.

Psychoanalytic interpretation tends to break down the end product, the art work, into primitive fantasy which has not yet been worked over by rational thought and been endowed with reality-tested derivations. It can provide enlightenment in the way in which one work of fiction can throw light upon another: analogies drawn between stories may suggest explanations omitted from others, or unexpected allusions, or unnoticed patterns. On the other hand, the (hypothetical) primitive fantasy may be irrelevant to the work and the psychoanalytic 'interpretation' no more than a distraction. When the fantastic imagination is influenced by psychoanalytic theory the challenge literary fantasy presents to psychoanalytic theory, and vice versa, is deadened. Thus Ursula LeGuin's *Earthsea* triology lacks, for all its charm and vividness, any real investigative power, because the story she tells is an embodiment of Jung's theories of the role of the shadow self and of death in the completed self. On a lesser plane, Philip Roth's short novel *The Breast* (1973) is in the tradition of transformation fantasy established by Gogol's 'The Nose' (1836) and Kafka's 'Metamorphosis' (1915), but, unlike his predecessors, Roth treats the transformation of David Alan Kepesh into an enormous pleasure-craving (originally pleasure-giving) breast as the realisation of a primitive fantasy. The psychoanalytic story is this: the initial form of love is not wanting to have someone (or some thing), but wanting to be someone (or something), and when the love-object is lost, there can be a regression to love as identification, so that the man who longs for the breast and cannot have it, or cannot have it in the way he wants it, replaces this desire with the desire to be the breast. This would be the explanation of David Alan Kepesh's hallucination, if it were a hallucination. David wants to discover that his transformation is a fantasy, but the novel accepts the premises of the unconscious: what is desired is, or strives to be, considered as fulfilled. The straightforward presentation in the novel of unconscious logic has extremely limited interest. True to Freudian theory, libidinous desires are seen not as procreative urges, but as organ satisfaction, and though the realisation is comic, it is maimed by its subservience to analytic dogma.

In 'Metamorphosis' Kafka uses Gregor's transformation into a gigantic insect to explore the logic of Gregor's situation. His family depends upon him, but their dependence is exploitation. His employers demand from him petty obedience and reliability. In becoming an insect, it is clear that Gregor has been treated like an insect. The disgust he arouses as an insect focuses the responses he usually arouses. After all, when his family discover an enormous insect in his room, they do not suppose that the monster has destroyed Gregor but immediately know that it is Gregor. And from Gregor's viewpoint, too, his thoughts are little changed: he wonders whether he can still catch his train, or whether the transformation provides an excuse for tardiness. The absence of shock or protest on Gregor's part enforces the awesome normality of the event. The absurdity and pathos of his defeat are so well integrated with his reality that the transformation can be accepted as literal and, at the same time, as a dramatisation of what is, in effect, happening to him in ordinary life. His family is ashamed, not pained or terrified, for this fantastic change effects only a slight shift in their daily patterns; it is an inconvenience. The transformation from 'they are treating him as an insect' to 'they are dealing with an insect' invites deeper development of both the family's attitudes and Gregor's abject state. The subsequent diminution of human qualities is a logical development of his pathetic situation; he becomes the creature he is seen to be.

In 'The Nose' Gogol's victim, Collegiate Assessor Kovalev, unlike Gregor Samsa, openly protests against the loss of his nose and its transformation into a military gentleman. He appeals to the law, to common sense, to his own self-importance; none of these would have aided Kafka's character. Thus Gogol's tale is free from the pathos that accepts cruel defeat as normal. Yet here we confront an event that is not merely empirically impossible but also incoherent. What, after all, does it mean to say that a nose has been transformed into a military gentleman? Did it grow like a sketch in a cartoon? Was it moulded like clay? Any suggestion, however, fails to explain how both Kovalev and the police inspector recognise the military gentleman as Kovalev's nose; we cannot imagine what such a recognition would be like.

'The Nose' can be read as a variation on both the double and castration themes, with the nose in the guise of a military gentleman representing the projection of Kovalev's ideal self, threatening him through competition and depriving him of his *raison d'être* by being a better version of himself. Kovalev's initial worry that without the nose he will be unable to visit the ladies implicates the castration theme, but it also involves vanity and pretence, which may be linked but not reduced to the castration theme. Indeed, to treat 'The Nose' as an allegory about the castration fear is not only to diminish the comedy with a pretence of explicitness but also to insult the careful probing of which psychoanalysis is capable. In 'A Supplement to Freud's "History of an Infantile Neurosis" ' (1928) Ruth Mack Brunswick analyses a non-fictional obsession wth the nose, from which Freud's Wolf-Man suffered as an sexual desires towards his father but, simultaneously, feared the castrating implications of this identification) alone can show how he used his delusions about nasal disfigurement to identify himself with his mother and wife (a mother-surrogate) and hence developed ideas of persecution, maintaining that a doctor's treatment of his nose resulted in disfigurement, or castration.

To interpret Gogol's tale without reference to any such material is to use analysis as a superficial glossary. Indeed, one could complain that an obvious psychoanalytic interpretation is objectionable because it is insufficiently 'Freudian'. However the complaint is focused, Kovalev's narcissism cannot be specified in psychoanalytic terms (as is the Wolf-Man's narcissism, directed as it is seen to be on his genitals and therefore emerging in terror as it conflicts with his identification with the woman) but indicates a more general (or, at least, less genital) self-love and blindness. The vulgar absurdity of his loss celebrates the absurdity of Kovalev's interests and suppositions and maliciously disrupts his complacency. The genital implications enforce the anxiety which might be mitigated by the implausibility of the narrative, but they do not make explicit the 'true' story.

'The Nose' presents ordinary self-interest, and the assumptions which spring from it, as belonging to an insane world. Gogol also exploits this theme in his 'Diary of a Madman' (1834) in which madness develops as a protest against normality. The aims and interests of Gogol's Madman are indeed absurd, but the normal world endorses them, thus also manifesting absurdity. The equation of the ordinary and the insane intensifies the difficulties in each world. Aims and interests become absurd when they cannot be satisfied in reality but are nonetheless supported by external factors. Frustration can lead to the inability to function in reality; when hallucinations become dominant, they indicate adult. A history of the patient's concern with his nose — he had been teased for his pug-nose as a schoolboy; he had suffered during puberty from a nasal catarrh which had caused sores on his nose and upper lip, he had been treated by the doctor who was later to treat him for gonorrhoea and who prescribed a salve which caused acne; yet the patient, while living in Vienna during the German occupation, had learned to appreciate the non-Hebraic appearance of his nose, and had also admired the perfection of his own nose in contrast to those of his wife and his mother, both of whom had warts on their noses — and of the material brought forward in his previous analysis, (when it became clear that the patient tended to identify himself with the woman in order to satisfy his that the aims, and interests have not been relinquished.

The narrator in Gogol's 'Diary' is, from the beginning, paranoid: 'At eight o'clock I set off for the office. The head of the department pretended he hadn't seen me come in. I played the same game, just as if we were strangers.'[9] Initially it is not difficult to detect the normal event within the description: the head of department might be lazy or aloof, and not bother to greet the man, but he is not playing what would normally be considered a game. Gradually, however, the narration clouds any rational interpretation: 'Today is Wednesday, and that's why I went to see the head of our department in his office. I made sure I got there early and sat down to sharpen all the quills.'[10] The glib but fragmented explanation of his eagerness is accompanied by an anxious yet hopelessly inadequate probing of others' characters: 'Our Director must be a very clever man: his study is full of shelves crammed with books [. . .] Really, he must have a very fine brain! He doesn't say much, but you can sense his mind is working the whole time.'[11]

The narrator's admiration is based upon his supposition that the Director is occupied by profound thoughts. Unable to discover the precise nature of these thoughts, he feels threatened — and so his ridiculous admiration increases his paranoia. It is his fear of not understanding what is going on around him (a justified fear, given his tendency to distortion) that leads him to suppose the dogs are speaking to one another and, subsequently, that they are exchanging letters. He wants to learn the thoughts (especially those concerning him) of the Director's daughter. He has no evidence that she has any thoughts about him whatsoever, but ignorance is intolerable. Since he must create evidence, he chooses the dogs as informers able to witness what is forbidden to him. The interception of the dog's letters (and, by this time, we are completely out of touch with his actual surroundings; presumably the woman does have a dog, but there is no clue as to what the narrator does to the dog, or how he gets a 'letter' from it) begins as a wish-fulfilment since the Director's daughter's dog speaks favourably of him. Yet, a moment later, the dog 'speaks' derogatively of him, claiming that the girl is always laughing at him. The one possibility he cannot accept is the most probable one: that the girl never thinks about him (though, from the narrator's viewpoint, such indifference is tantamount to a direct attack). The narrator rejects the dog's description of the woman's attitude, concluding that the dog is jealous of him, and, simultaneously and contradictorily, that the head of his department is responsible for the girl's derision.

Eventually the narrator's testing of reality works upon this principle: if something might be the case, and if he himself is not persuaded otherwise, then it is the case. He wonders what prevents him from being the King of Spain, and subsequently 'realises' that he is the King of Spain. Reality-testing is the aim of his fantasy, but because this (primary) aim is thwarted, Gogol's diarist is locked within his own fears and wishes.

The sense of absurdity which arises because the world itself — that is our perceptions of it — has no coherence, or because, although the world is coherent and predictable, its coherence is experienced as absurd, is linked to an anxiety about what is hidden and may be found. The nature of objectivity itself is in doubt, either because the perceiver cannot test reality or because circumstances themselves are arbitrary. Awkwardness and embarrassment frequently dominate the fantasy in which absurdity and anxiety operate, since awkwardness arises from (in many cases, quite literally) not knowing one's way around. Student Anselmus, in Hoffmann's 'The Golden Pot', is always stumbling against things, forgetting the time, spoiling and losing things, because his imagination obliterates his actual surroundings. Throughout, he is tormented by the inability to demarcate fantasy from reality. As a consequence, neither's characteristics make sense to him.

Embarrassment is utilised in fantasy literature not only to mark the commonly experienced sense of awkwardness, but also the way in which value-priorities can be ridiculously altered: thus Joseph K., just prior to being executed, weeps with embarrassment for the artist who is reluctant to inscribe the tombstone. Embarrassment arises from a compulsive clownishness, or sympathy with clownishness, when, in all reason, concern with form and composure should give way to other considerations.

Kafka is a master in conjoining these fantasy themes. He describes the inability to gain mastery over anything. The opening sentence of 'A Country Doctor' (1919) reads very much like an anxiety dream:

> I was in great perplexity; I had to start on an urgent journey; a seriously ill patient was waiting for me in a village ten miles off: a thick blizzard of snow filled all the wide spaces between him and me; I had a gig, a light gig with big wheels, exactly right for our country roads; muffled in furs, my bag of instruments in my hand, I was in the courtyard all ready for the journey; but there was no horse to be had, no horse.[12]

The doctor learns that his own horse has died in the night, and the servant girl tries without success to borrow one in the village. From this impasse the dream-like sequences gain impetus. A groom brings forth two large horses and asks whether he should yoke them up. When the servant girl Rose goes to help him, the groom bites her face. The doctor shouts at him, but then realises that no one else would help him. As though guessing his regret, the groom takes no offence. He directs the doctor into the gig, declaring that he will stay with the servant girl. Rose shrieks and runs into the house. The groom claps his hands, the horses charge forward, and as the gig departs the doctor hears his front door being broken down by the groom.

The doctor is immediately transported to the patient's house. The patient whispers to him, 'Let me die,' but the doctor persists in believing that nothing is wrong with the man. He decides to leave, hoping to return in time to help Rose, but he soon realises that patient is truly ill. In his flesh is a hand-sized wound filled by rose-coloured worms with small white heads and many legs. The patient, a young man, now pleads, 'Will you save me?' and the doctor thinks, 'That is what all patients are like, always whining, always expecting the impossible from me.' The family and the village elders warn him that if he does not heal the young man they will kill him. They strip the doctor's clothes and place him into bed beside the patient. The young man complains that the doctor is taking up too much room in the bed, and then assures him that his wound is not very bad, if only one adopts a wider perspective. The doctor attempts escape, but the previously swift horses, now drag at a snail's pace. Time itself is static and motion impossible; the doctor cannot even retrieve the coat sleeve caught in the gig.

Kafka's summary of the moral is: 'A false-alarm on the night-bell once answered — it can never be made good, not ever.'[13] The doctor's will, however, always in abeyance, deprives him of the judgement as to how he might have heeded the warning. The paralysis of will is not merely one dream characteristic in its own right, but develops from the inconsistencies of the doctor's responses and thoughts. On arrival at the patient's home he clings to the opinion that the patient is not seriously ill, yet he had behaved as though he were embarking upon an urgent journey. The realisation of the gravity of the patient's illness is rapidly metamorphosised into his own danger: the patient cancels his plea for the doctor to save him (which is itself a cancellation of his initial plea to let him die) with the assurance that the wound is not so bad, if only one employs a wider vision; but this reassurance occurs when the doctor is in bed with the patient, therefore his partner, and himself facing the prospect of death (because he will be killed if he does not save the young man). The doctor is the victim and therefore helpless, but he is also guilty of having left Rose to be the groom's victim; thus the worms crawling in the wound are, as is the wound itself, rose-coloured.

In this circumstance, anxiety as a response to external circumstances is superficially rational: the doctor must get to his patient, but is deprived of the means of travelling. Moreover, he must save the patient or die, yet he knows the patient cannot be saved. While appalled at the groom's behaviour, he is afraid to forfeit his help. Although he wants to help Rose, he is detained first by the sick man's family, and then by the recalcitrant horses. These conflicts generate anxiety because the circumstances are absurdly fragmented and change so rapidly that the doctor cannot integrate them. First he is detained, then unwillingly accelerated towards his destination, subsequently detained and threatened, and finally captivated in timelessness with no capacity for movement.

The shifting, uncontrolled circumstances show what it is like to be unable to make a decision: these changes impede judgement because they impede the ability to make predictions upon which decisions must be based. Yet even in refusing to decide, one is caught up in events, one performs various actions, while the world goes by so quickly one cannot understand what is happening. Alternatively, the inability to take charge of one's actions leads to an awful impasse, making any action impossible, making even occurrences impossible. 'A Country Doctor' reveals the risks we take every day as well as the impact of our hesitance to take risks. Guilt arises from the inability to master this awful reality. It is generated by lack of control, self-doubt and confusion. In desiring the safety of detachment, one discovers the terrifying fact of involvement alongside helplessness. Thus guilt, normally linked with accountability of action, is here tied to helplessness: the doctor is helpless as he leaves Rose with the cruel groom; he is helpless confronting the patient's infected wound; and, ultimately he is helplessly bound by time. Yet the allegations against him, and the self-accusations are consistent with Kafka's presentation of morality as a psychological nightmare. In *The Trial* guilt is based upon accusation, while in 'The Judgement' it is based upon mockery and rejection. In both works guilt thrives upon the need for and impossibility of certainty. In 'A Country Doctor' guilt is more closely linked, as it would be in an ordinary moral framework, to consequences of actions, but the consequences of actions (or inaction) are seen in a context in which responsibility cannot be attributed. The sense of guilt arises from the intersection of fear, sympathy and self-doubt. The doctor is, like Wakefield, in the midst of human concerns, but unable to influence them. For his insignificance and helplessness he feels responsible, and, in some respects, is responsible, yet he knows there is nothing he can do about it. He, like Wakefield, excludes himself from the human arena. His exclusion is a punishment for his guilt and at the same time it is the object of his guilt. Thus he is trapped. Helpessness marks him as guilty for an inadequacy he cannot master, and also makes him behave badly, thus compounding his guilt. Moreover, his helplessness arises from the nature of his circumstances which make decision and action either impossible or ineffective.

A successor to Kafka who uses anxiety derived from anxiety dreams to investigate guilt is Delmore Schwartz. In the title story of *In Dreams Begin Responsibilities* Schwartz uses the scenario of a son watching a film of his parents' courtship, a fantastical device which presents controlled and purposive reflection, much as Dickens's use of the ghosts in 'A Christmas Carol' forces memories upon Scrooge, for whom reflection and reconsideration would be inconsistent. The technique in both works is perfectly suited to the authors' respective purposes, but in neither does the fantastical device result in a fantastic tale; the reconsiderations, the comments and realisations, stand firmly within the realist tradition.

In 'The Track Meet' from the same collection, however, Schwartz uses a dream as a kind of theatre in which conventional assumptions crumble, and thus leads us across the threshold of fantasy. Frank Lawrence, the narrator in 'The Track Meet', is accustomed to entertaining English visitors. He learns that an explanation of American customs in terms of the 'rules of the game' or 'fair play' satisfies their curiosity. He also realises that Englishmen regard emotional behaviour by spectators as a display in accord with rules, as part of the game they watch. Very early one morning, Reginald Law visits Frank Lawrence without warning and without apology. Awkward in his unexpected presence, Frank finds conversation difficult: 'In these circumstances,' he confesses, 'I have often said foolish, and indiscreet, or intimate, or tactless things, merely to revive conversation, being made panicky by painful silences and feeling wrongly that the responsibility is always mine.'[14] As though puzzled by his host's reticence, Reginald Law asks, 'You *are* Frank Lawrence?' and then asks permission to call him 'Frank' — an unusual request, the narrator reflects, from an Englishman.

Reginald Law declares that they are to attend a track meet. Though Frank insists that no track meet would be held at this early hour, they proceed to the stadium. At the entrance Frank asks to shake Law's hand: 'Do you want to be sure I don't have a knife up my sleeve?' Reginald asks. Frank, however, merely wants to dispel the persistent feeling that he is dreaming.

Inside the stadium Frank sees his mother sitting in a box. He is not pleased to see her and hopes that she will not notice him. Among the men taking part in the race are his five brothers. He tells Law that they are all named after the crowned heads of Europe, and that his real name is Franz Joseph. Law says that he had been told Frank was an only child. Frank wonders whether their mutual friend had told Law this on the basis of Frank's egoism. Yet he does now seem to be an only child: 'I called out to my brothers, and they stopped, turned, and looked at me and then looked blankly at each other, as if they did not recognise me, or as if I were some crackpot who was pretending to be a friend of the performers.'[15] Reginald Law tells Frank not to worry — an injunction which only confuses and frightens him: how does Law know he is worried, and why might he be worried? Frank's shouting draws attention. His mother looks at him coldly, without recognition. He appeals to his brother Nicholas (whom the family called the Czar), who is especially fond of him, but the brother continues to jog unperturbed. In desperation Frank cries, 'You used to like me very much. When I die, you will be silent.'

The hundred yard dash begins. His two brothers keep up with the front runner. One brother tackles the front runner, allowing the second brother to win the race:

'That's nepotism,' I said, rising to my feet to see what was happening. 'I mean that's not fair — that's against the rules of the game.'

'Nature is unfair,' said Law, 'and existence is also unfair. There is too much pointless pretence. That fellow who you seem to think is your brother behaved according to the dictates of his heart, clearly. Most human beings behave like that and don't admit it — not even to themselves.'

As for me, I must admit my feelings were mixed; I was touched by Carlos's brotherly action, however unfair.[16]

The mother kisses the winning brother and says, 'You have brought honour on your family.'

Frank and Reginald occupy themselves reading a newspaper account of various atrocities. The one-mile race begins as a girl in a bathing suit climbs on to the track. Frank, trying to express his outrage appropriately, insists that this is not the 'done thing', that it spoils the game. 'You are interested in platitudes,' Law replies, 'but I am interested in reality.' The pretty girl tries to distract the pace-setter by kissing him. When this does not work, she hits him over the head with a pop bottle. Now the brothers begin to quarrel among themselves. Frank tries to climb on to the track to prevent a family riot, but he halts when 'an official who looked like a senator or the governor of a state — florid, heavy, and histrionic' signals two policemen, who raise their rifles and shoot down the winner of the race:

> 'I don't want to be killed,' I said to myself, drawing back.
> 'Don't you want to join your brothers?' asked Law [. . .]' Don't you think you should?'
> 'No,' I said, in answer to everything.[17]

Frank Lawrence tries to run away as the boys on the track are shot down. Law holds him back and tells him that he will not be able to escape, but Frank replies that it does not matter, because he knows it is all a dream:

> 'What difference does it make if it is a dream or it is not a dream?' he said coldly and sternly as I burst into hysterical, grotesque, and unmanly tears. 'It is worse for you — it is far worse for you if it *is* a dream. I should think that by this time you would know that.'
> He stood above me, glaring and looking as if he still intended to keep me from getting up from the ground where I sprawled. The dusk was growing above the empty stadium, and the cold sky looked like a distant lake ringed by black and leafless trees.
> How is it worse for me if it is a dream and only a dream?'
> 'I detest explanation,' said Law. 'Do you insist on one? Are you really sure you don't understand?'
> 'I often feel that I know little or nothing,' I said in a pleading voice, fearful that I would soon awaken, and that the moment of awakening would occur just as he began to tell me what I wanted to know so much.
> 'The things I read you out of the paper were, if anything, more shocking than what has just occurred down there on the field. You don't escape from nightmare by waking up, you know. And if what occurred on the field were merely imaginary and unreal and merely your own private hallucination, then the evil that has terrified you is rooted in your own mind and heart. Like the rest of us,' Law said scornfully, 'you not only know more than you think you know but more than you are willing to admit. Look at yourself! *Just look at yourself!*'
> I tried once more to stand up, and awoke, and found myself standing up, staring, in a sweat of confusion and dread, not at the sky

but at the looking glass above the chest of drawers next to my
dishevelled bed. The face I saw was livid and swollen with barbarous
anger and unbearable shame. [18]

Delmore Schwartz, in trying to extend the ordinary notion of guilt,
insists, in the wake of psychoanalysis (which greatly interested him) that
dreams, or fantasies in general — for Frank Lawrence's vision is far too
elaborate and coherent to be treated as an actual dream — are linked to
our own desires and aims. Thus Schwartz indicates how psychoanalysis
does not, as its emphasis on the determination of thought and feeling
might imply, mitigate guilt, but rather enforces it: we are responsible for
our dreams (as we are for mistakes, slips of the tongue, 'unintentional'
actions) because they express what we are, what we desire, what we
unconsciously aim to do. But Schwartz's extension of the concept of guilt
is impeded by his confused and crude presentation of the source of Frank
Lawrence's guilt. For if we are responsible for our nightmares, we are
certainly not responsible for them in the way in which we are responsible
for our actions. Unconscious impulses, desires, fears and aims must be
recognised as part of the self, but to base accusations upon them as though
they were actions is to remove, as Kafka does, guilt from its ordinary
context, but without tracing a new logic. Kafka shows how fear,
timidity and uncertainty dominate a character's life, shape it and, usually,
damage it. For this destructiveness, whether it is a reaction to another
person or to an external attack or to internal fears, the character is
responsible, and for this he must be punished. The punishment is often
seen not in terms of the consequences of an action but as a description of
it; in these actions, in these responses, the person discovers his nature; this
discovery and this possession constitute his punishment. And, pathetically
combined with responsibility for one's impoverishment, is a timid but
abiding self-love. In Kafka's meditation 'Unhappiness' the narrator, like
Frank Lawrence, recognises that his terror arises from the terror within
him. He tells a neighbour that he has just seen a ghost in his room, and
the neighbour replies that if one does not believe in ghosts, one need not
be afraid if one turns up. The narrator says, 'Oh, that's only a secondary
fear. The real fear is a fear of what caused the apparition. And that fear
doesn't go away . . . All the same . . . if you steal my ghost from me all is
over between us, for ever.' [19]

Reginald Law's assertions that Frank, like everyone else, does what he
wants to do and that he, like everyone else, knows more than he wants to
admit, together with the concluding command, '*Just look at yourself*!'
wield a schoolmaster's cane rather than a moral hammer; yet what

Schwartz does succeed in doing very well is to present an original example of egoism, and to link egoism to timidity and self-abasement rather than to self-aggrandisement. Frank Lawrence's initial fear with Reginald Law, that he will be indiscreet in an attempt to make conversation, is not only an obvious fear of self-confrontation, but also a fear of making his thoughts appear ridiculous and therefore unimportant. This precisely is how he appears to his family in the stadium. His mother ignores him and praises the brother who won the race. His brothers ignore him, and think him a clown as he tries to get their attention. Their cold behaviour registers fairly what he is, for he flees as they are being shot down on the track. The true egoist is both neglected and neglecting — or perhaps another term is needed here, for Schwartz's picture of the egoist is of a person who cares for his own safety, but who does not care about himself. Even Frank Lawrence's desire to understand what is going on, in the sense of understanding what it means, indicates animal fear rather than intellectual curiosity. He wakes to escape Reginald's command to take a look at himself, and of course discovers that he does not escape the nightmare by waking. The over-written conclusion (the face he sees in the mirror is 'livid and swollen with barbarous anger and unbearable shame') undermines Schwartz's success in depicting a character in the process of becoming more and more passively egoistic, while self-respect and sympathy struggle feebly and vainly for realisation. A violent puritanical reaction of the waking self against the unconscious or possible self destroys the delicate gropings towards self-knowledge which Schwartz had previously depicted.

In fantasy literature most anxiety dreams, or portrayals of waking life as similar to anxiety dreams, explore the disintegration of commonplace expectations, with the disintegrating forces working according to new and hostile laws. Friedrich Dürrenmatt's novel *Once a Greek* . . . [20] (1966) however carefully traces the growth of anxiety from propitious rather than unfortunate conditions. Wish-fulfilment is seen to be alarming not because, as in certain fairy tales, we wish for things we do not want, but because any divergence of known order is threatening.

The protagonist of *Once a Greek* . . . is Arnolph Archilochus who, at the age of 45, works as an assistant to an assistant bookkeeper in the Obstetrical Forceps Division of a large Swiss engineering company. Within his meagre and sordid surroundings he seeks to confirm his dedication to mental and physical purity, and places various hero figures in his own hierarchy of the ethical cosmos. Longing for a mate, he places an advertisement in the newspaper 'Greek seeks Greek wife.' He has, in fact, never visited the home of his ancestors, but he thrills at the travel posters depicting that land and believes he must make his home with a native of Greece. Chloë Saloniki answers the advertisement and meets him in his usual restaurant. She is beautiful and, apparently, wealthy, and immediately falls in love with Archilochus. As he walks through the city with her the people who form the hierarchy of his ethical cosmos greet him with friendly respect. The following day his superiors at the engineering works praise him for his reports, though they mention reports he has not written. The director of the company, in what he calls an act of creative socialism, plans to make Archilochus director of the Atomic Cannon Division. Despite his pacifist beliefs, Archilochus is delighted; but everything turns sour as he recognises an abstract painting consisting of two ellipses and a parabola as a nude portrait of his Chloë. The artist, however, manages to distract him by asking him to undress and suggestion that he pose as Mars.

Archilochus's good fortune continues. Chloë's employers have made their large house over to her, and she and Archilochus plan to marry. Immediately after the ceremony, however, Archilochus realises that his luck has been engineered by Chloë's many former lovers. He runs away, terrified by disillusion. It was the established system that promoted and polluted Archilochus's good fortune. Suspecting that Archilochus will want to revenge himself upon them, the revolutionaries (who have also been Chloë's lovers) visit him in his garret and offer him a grenade. The revolutionary leader tells Archilochus that the existing order has made a fool of him and that he should now assassinate the President, who formerly stood high in Archilochus's hierarchy. Archilochus climbs the imposing frieze along the side of the presidential palace, and when he accosts the President he is greeted warmly. The President tells him that the world is hypocritical and evil; only love can mitigate these conditions. Thus he advises him to devote himself to Chloë. Archilochus tries to follow this advice, but he cannot find Chloë. He travels to Greece, which disappoints him, but discovers Chloë while digging at an archaeological site.

The main thrust of the novel is political, with Archilochus's personal happiness contrasted with the dilapidation and sordidness of his surroundings until it becomes clear that the human forces behind his poverty are also manipulating, for their own ends, his happier circumstances. But a highly interesting element in the drama is the way the elaboration of wish-fulfilment leads directly into nightmare via reality-testing. The enormity of Archilochus's unhappiness — that is, the extent of Chloë's promiscuity — is as fantastic as the extent of his former happiness. In effect, then, the turn away from wish-fulfilment is not a turn towards realism but towards another outlandish construction which reveals the anxiety inherent in the notion of wish-fulfilment. Laws and other generalities operate such that, within a very wide and varying range, certain reasons or explanations of events and actions can be given, whereas other proffered explanations are nonsensical. If these flexible but reasonably recognisable generalities are systematically or continuously broken, apparently in our favour, then some personal (and therefore arbitrary) force may be at work. Since the force is arbitrary it may turn against us, and since normal laws and reasons have been superseded by that force, we have no means of predicting its course. We may be as easily caught out by the new order as favoured by it. Or, for reasons as hidden as its rules of operation, it may cease to function, or give way to a nasty strategy.

A psychoanalytic interpretation of the phenomena of the immediate fulfilment of wishes would refer to an infantile belief in the omnipotence of thought. The immediate realisation of wishes would probably conflict with other needs and desires. A child, for example, might wish a parent dead, but also recognise his dependence and fear the parent's death. In this case, too, anxiety would arise from reality-testing, or imaginative elaboration of wish, but the important difference is that the fantasised forces are predictable: one's wishes are the forces at work. Anxiety arises from the fantasised extent of power, and from the ambivalence of one's wishes. Dürrenmatt, however, depicts immediate and unexplained fulfilment of wishes in a context in which one has no power and no means of making predictions. Investigation of the particular fantasy he employs reveals the immediate fulfilment of wishes as a sign that one is trapped in another's plot. Unexplained patterns, whether favourable or disappointing, indicate individual paralysis. When one must depend upon wish-fulfilment to gain satisfaction, one is already hopelessly frustrated and therefore even satisfaction will generate anxiety.

6 The Fantasy of Order: Vladimir Nabokov

Vladimir Nabokov's contributions to fantasy literature have not, previously, been adequately appreciated. The over-used, and inaccurately used, adjective 'Kafkaesque' has been applied to some of his work, but Nabokov himself insists, with justification, that he was not influenced by Kafka and, more importantly, that his work bears no similarity to Kafka's. In his introduction to the American edition of *Bend Sinister* (1963), after issuing his usual warning to Freudians — 'Keep Out' — Nabokov declares that an automatic comparison between his novel 'and Kafka's creations or Orwell's clichés would go merely to prove that the automaton could not have read either the great German writer or the mediocre English one'. Kafka's fantasies are explorations of emotional conditions; their logic is the logic of psychology and their aim is to present a literal account of what is happening subjectively to his characters. Nabokov uses fantasy to emphasise the fragmentation of normal perception, to deny the sense of order, to insist that logic and order are themselves fantasies. Thus Nabokov has more affinity to Jorge Luis Borges, who creates orders which are preposterous and yet compelling.

Bend Sinister is a marvellous novel, and reaches the border of fantasy in its combination of cruelty and comedy arising from misconceived aims and ridiculously imbalanced priorities; but the nightmares are registered with a severe and steadfast morality; the mishaps and mischances are the result of stupidity and insensitivity, and though Adam Krug's world becomes abnormal, his judgement remains sound. Nabokov protects Krug from the loss of his son with the insistence that he is a fictional character, and thus not subject to the actual slings of fortune; but this reprieve does not change the issues of the narrative or the concepts therein employed, all of which fall within the realistic tradition. To be reminded that realism is an artifice is not to call the normality or stability of its terms into question.

In the tales now printed in *Nabokov's Quartet* (1967) we see Nabokov the fantasist brilliantly at work. 'An Affair of Honour', which is a fine tribute to Chekhov's 'The Duel', tells the story of Anton Petrovich, a Russian émigré living in Berlin, who goes to Kassel on business, is delayed, but then returns to Berlin without notifying his wife. When he arrives at his apartment he discovers their friend Berg standing in front of the bedroom mirror, putting on his tie. Anton Petrovich challenges Berg to a duel and directs his wife to leave their home. On the way to the duelling place Anton Petrovich flees and hides in an hotel. There he dreams of a reconciliation with his wife and of his honour being saved through Berg's own defection from the duel. He dreams, too, of the ham sandwiches his wife used to make him, with the fat hanging over the edge of the bread. He orders a ham sandwich from the hotel, and the tale concludes as he eats it.

The fantastic aspect of 'An Affair of Honour' arises from the way in which the order and stability of the external world are overpowered by the confusion and fragmentation of perceptions. Indeed, when the external world is described in terms of perceptions, which, ordinarily, are thought to provide adequate information, the most fundamental presuppositions about external objects and other people are abandoned. When Anton Petrovich is introduced to Berg, the man 'rose out of nonbeing, bowed in greeting, and settled down again — into an armchair instead of his previous nonbeing.'[1] His perception of Berg is, in Berkeleian fashion, a creation of Berg, and thus the fragile character of his perceptions indicates a fragilely constructed external world:

Anton Petrovich had some more vodka and the room went into a spin. The gliding chessboard seemed on the point to collide with the bottles; the bottles, together with the table, set off towards the couch; the couch with mysterious Adelaida Albertorna headed for the window; and the window also started to move. The accursed motion was somehow connected with Berg, and had to be stopped — stopped at once, trampled upon, torn, destroyed [. . .][2]

This is fantasy rather than a tale with a mad protagnoist because the arrangement of events, and the way in which events are discovered, is in total harmony with Anton Petrovich's confusion. His realisation of his wife's infidelity (' "Pink and moist," Anton Petrovich thought with fond anticipation, and he carried his bag on into the bedroom. In the bedroom, Berg was standing before the wardrobe mirror, putting on his tie.'[3]) indicates the ease, the naturalness, with which facts shatter expectations and desires. Anton Petrovich is not mad because he can see his expectations failing. As he goes through the motions of shooting practice (without a gun) he wonders how a pistol should be held: 'You are supposed to hold it like this and take aim. Or like this, perhaps, right up near your chin — it seems easier to do it this way. And at that instant, as he held before him the paperweight in the form of a parrot, pointing it this way and that, Anton Petrovich realised that he would be killed.'[4]

Anton Petrovich knows that reality will not match his needs, but this knowledge does not facilitate more effective reality-testing; instead, it forces him to make outlandish efforts to understand his position and to respond appropriately, even as he knows he is bound to destroy himself in so doing. He challenges Berg to a duel because, in his confusion at having discovered Berg in his bedroom, he has no idea how to respond; therefore he chooses a platitudinous and outdated role, from which Nabokov extracts a marvellous comedy. Anton Petrovich struggles to take off his glove; it is a new glove and therefore tight. He throws it, meaning to hit Berg, but it lands in a basin of water. 'Good shot,' Berg comments, and his wryness gauges the appropriate attitude towards Anton Petrovich's ridiculous pose, or pseudo-pose. But Anton Petrovich cannot share Berg's justifiable dismissal of his challenge because he cannot be casual about his wife's infidelity. How, then, in these sophisticated circumstances, can he express his anger and abashment? He must be histrionic, he must make some impact, but his choice of a role only increases the absurdity of his situation.

Nabokov superbly mingles the ridiculous and the fantastic. Aware that he is out of phase with reality, Anton Petrovich makes more and more attempts to get things right, resulting in more and more failures. His confusion is such that there is no longer any distinction between success and failure, because the resulting anxiety is such that a nearly impossible success is the only hope; yet it is not possible to believe in the impossible. After contacting his seconds Anton Petrovich returns to his apartment and lies down on the sofa: 'For some reason his left wrist felt uncomfortable. Oh, of course — my watch. He took it off and wound it, thinking at the same time, "Extraordinary, how this man retains his composure — does not even forget to wind his watch." At the same time Anton Petrovich knows that he has no control over the situation, and he tries to use this — his only certainty — to regain control: 'If I think that nothing will happen to me, then the worst will happen. Everything in life always happens the other way around. It would be nice to read something — for the last time — before going to sleep.' He immediately forgets his belief that everything happens the other way around, for he then sees this expectation as a prediction: "'There I go again,'" he moaned inwardly. "Why for the last time? I am in a terrible state. I must take hold of myself. Oh, if only I were given some sign. Cards?'"[5]

The inability to test reality, in conjunction with the sane knowledge that one cannot — but, simultaneously, that one needs to — test it, results in a profoundly ridiculous position. From the awareness of one's ludicrousness and of the compulsions which aggravate it, arises an abject, self-apologetic fear, a fantastic elaboration upon embarrassment. Anton Petrovich is on his way to the duelling place, momentarily reprieved by numbness: 'Only when the train jerked and began to move did his brain start working again, and in this instant he was possessed by the feeling that comes in dreams when, speeding along in a train from nowhere to nowhere, you suddenly realise that you are travelling clad only in your underpants.'[6]

In *The Interpretation of Dreams* Freud classifies such dreams among exhibition dreams. Being scantily clad stems from the childhood condition of being naked or near naked among many people without shame or embarrassment. This retrospective element is sufficient to identify the dream as a wish-fulfilment since, Freud concluded, the impressions of earliest childhood crave reproduction for their own sake, even perhaps without reference to their content.[7] The disagreeable sensation of the dream is a result of the censor's reaction to the presentation of the naked or partially dressed self: the unconscious desire is for the exhibition to proceed, while the demands of the censor require that it come to an end. Thus the dream presents the self as undressed, but also inhibited and ashamed. Freud drew links between his analysis of this type of dream and the significance in literature of nakedness. Hans Christian Anderson's 'The Emperor's New Clothes', in which the Emperor appears naked before all the people because he is afraid to admit that he cannot see the garment which is allegedly visible only to the good and the true, represents the condition realised in the dream; and in Book IX of the *Odyssey* the hero's appearing naked before Naussicaä expresses the man's understandable exhibitionist impulses towards a young woman.

Such interpretations, however, are irrelevant to Anton Petrovich's feeling that he is travelling clad only in his underpants, for it does not stem from a wish but from an assessment of his actual situation. His fantasised shame indicates his vulnerability in conjunction with his frantic determination to deny it; he must deny it because he believes that no one will help him. Thus isolated, he enters the fantastic world, which is essentially one of vulnerability because it is unknown or, at the very least, unpredictable. Embarrassment leads Anton Petrovich to deny this vulnerability, to pretend he does know how to respond and to behave — a pretence which leads him to create even more difficult circumstances, while the embarrassment perpetuates these circumstances. The imbalance of priorities which embarrassment induces in Anton Petrovich is enforced by his seconds. He takes one of his seconds aside and admits:

> 'You know, it's awfully silly, but you see, I don't know how to shoot, so to speak, I mean, I know how, but I've had no practice at all [...]'
> 'Hm,' said Mityushin, 'that's too bad. Today in Sunday, otherwise you could have had a lesson or two. That's really bad luck.'[8]

The moderate sympathy Mityushin offers the prospective duellist, and the acceptance of his plight that moderation implies, must be a shock to Anton Petrovich, yet he himself has established this standard. His fear thus becomes further isolated, while his musings are tortuous exercises for damping the fear through mastery of his embarrassment:

> 'I must dress soberly, but elegantly. Tuxedo? No, that would be idiotic. A black suit, then ... and yes, a black tie. The new black suit. But if there's a wound, a shoulder wound, say ... The suit will be ruined ... The blood, the hole, and besides, they may start cutting off the sleeve. Nonsense, nothing of the sort is going to happen. I must wear my new black suit. And when the duel starts, I shall turn up my jacket collar — that's the custom, I think [...] Now, there was a question: Does one salute one's opponent? What does Onegin do in the opera? Perhaps a discreet tip of the hat from a distance would be just right. Then they would probably start marking off the yards and loading the pistols. What would he do meanwhile? Yes, of course — he would place one foot on a stump somewhere a little off, and wait in a casual attitude. But what if Berg also put one foot on a stump? Berg was capable of it ... Mimicking me to embarrass me. That would be awful [...] Somebody (in a Pushkin story?) ate cherries from a paper bag. Yes, but you have to bring that bag to the duelling ground — looks silly.'[9]

Embarrassment, or anxiety at the prospect of embarrassment, here works as a defence against the crucial fear — the fear for his life, yet at the same time it clearly and cruelly works towards making that fear more realistic. Anton Petrovich's usual world becomes confused and fantastic when he learns of his wife's infidelity. Since normality becomes fantastic, he must respond with the creation of a fantasy, yet he knows — and the pathos of his ridiculousness springs from this knowledge — that his fantasy is maladjustive. Therefore he tries to revise it, improve it, reshape it, but he estranges himself further from reality. Yet, until the end of the tale, Anton Petrovich is not trying to escape through fantasy, but to find his way around a fantastic world.

The most conventional tale of fantasy in *Nabokov's Quartet* is 'The Visit to the Museum'. It is conventional in that it uses a common device of fantasy — the transformation of reality into an inescapable dream, though Nabokov uses the convention to present an unusual paradox. The narrator plans to spend two or three days at Montsiert. Before he leaves Paris a friend asks him to look for his grandfather's portrait in the city museum and to discover whether it can be purchased. The narrator believes that his friend has simply made up the story about the portrait and is determined (since, in any case, he detests museums) to find some excuse not to perform the errand. As he walks through Montsiert, however, it begins to rain, and he takes shelter in what he discovers to be the doorway of the museum. He goes inside and, to his surprise, finds the portrait of his friend's grandfather. When he asks the museum's director whether it can be purchased, the director denies that there is such a painting in the museum. When the narrator leads him to it the director refuses to make a decision about selling the painting, since there is no record of it. He leads the narrator to his office, through the museum which now appears enormous. The narrator soon loses the director and wanders through strange display rooms and corridors. Eventually he discovers an exit, but his relief is eclipsed by the discovery that he has stepped into Russia — not the Russia of his youth, but (he discovers from the modern lettering on a sign) Soviet Russia, where he is an outlaw. He must destroy all evidence of his illegal self — his identification papers, his foreign money, and even his clothes. The narrator refuses to relate the details of his arrest and his eventual escape: 'Suffice it to say that it cost me incredible patience and effort to get back abroad, and that, ever since, I have foresworn carrying out commissions entrusted one by the insanity of others.'[10]

In 'The Visit to the Museum' Nabokov appears to tease Freudians. As well as scatological displays there are exhibits of a more delicately symbolic nature: the room filled with musical instruments, in the centre of which is a pool, the room of fountains and brooks with its slippery, windy edges, combined with the impression of *déja vu*, are open temptations to interpret the museum as the womb (Freud suggests that the impression of *déja vu* in dreams always refers to the mother's genitals, as a place we have all been before), though perhaps Nabokov wishes to indicate that his narrator has been trapped within a Freudian nightmare. In any case, the museum is not the womb, and the tale is not allegorical, but based upon the paradox of being trapped within someone else's fantasy even as the truth or the significance of that fantasy is denied. It is logically impossible to have another person's dream, in the same way it is impossible to have another person's pain. The only coherent description of such an occurrence involves the empirical impossibility of having a dream exactly like — identical in character to — another's. But this is not what happens in 'The Visit to the Museum'. The dream is shared, not because it captivates the narrator's attention or appeals to him or even repels him, but because it has, alongside its thoroughly dream-like character, the logic of reality. Thus Nabokov defies the formulation of Delmore Schwartz — that our dreams arise from ourselves and that we are therefore responsible for them.

This tale's uncanniness can be accounted for in terms of Freud's theory of the uncanny: it refers to, and stimulates, the (discarded) belief that dreams have the same status as external events; yet the applicability of the theory merely indicates the facet that the tale does contain uncanny effects, and uncanny effects do not alone make a good fantasy tale. Indeed, because 'The Visit to the Museum' merely focuses on the possible doubt as to the distinction between dream and reality, without revealing anything new within that doubt, and without using that doubt to indicate any reality, its cleverness is underemployed.

Nabokov's novel *The Defence*(1930), like 'An Affair of Honour', is a humorous and persuasive celebration of the ridiculous, with confusion used to register normality: the order that we accept as normal can, in reality, be maintained only through fantasy; normality must be ordered, but to believe in order is madness.

The story centres around Aleksandr Ivanovich Luzhin, a master-chess-player who grew up in pre-Soviet Russia. His father, a writer of children's books, is disturbed by the boy's strangeness, but hopes that his peculiarity indicates genius, and dreams of creeping downstairs one night to discover Luzhin performing on the piano like a virtuoso. (A woodcut of a father in a nightshirt observing a boy at the piano appears in the adult Luzhin's flat — presumably the father's fantasy was based upon this sentimental picture.) Expecting to hear praise of his son's abilities, the father instead learns from the headmaster that young Luzhin is listless and lazy and, what is more important, does not join in games with the other boys.

Luzhin's parents hold a musical evening in honour of his mother's father, who was a (neglected) composer. The child, when urged to join the company, retreats to his father's study where he overhears the violinist's telephone conversation with a jealous mistress. During the conversation the violinist toys with a small chess-set on the desk. Discovering the boy's presence he asks whether Luzhin plays the game and then, in a languorous but enticing manner, speaks of the subtle and superb harmonies of chess. Still ignorant of how to play, Luzhin takes the chess-set into his room and eventually persuades his young aunt (while the house is in an uproar over his mother's jealousy about the father's attachment to her sister) to teach him the rudiments of the game. He plays truant from school to visit his aunt, hoping she will instruct him further. Instead, she uses Luzhin as a decoy for an elderly admirer, who plays chess with Luzhin as she slips away. The father learns of the truancy, and then of the reasons for it. Impressed, he seeks the advice of a chess-playing neighbour, who confirms that the boy has a remarkable talent. Luzhin begins to play in tournaments and travels with his teacher Valentinov, who abandons him when he thinks that Luzhin is outgrowing his appeal as a prodigy. Luzhin continues to play, and now travels alone. At a spa where he is resting in preparation for a match with Turati — a younger player, with a reputation for being more daring than Luzhin — he meets a young woman, who, like himself, is a Russian émigré. They become engaged. During the tournament he collapses, and his doctors advise him not to play chess again, lest the excitement precipitate another breakdown. His wife tries to arrange his surroundings so as to avoid all references to chess, though she cannot insult him by cutting out the chess pages of the newspaper. Luzhin understands the game people are playing with him sufficiently to pretend not to notice these pages, but he memorises the positions and mentally solves the problems. Moreover, he discovers a small chess-set in the lining of an old jacket and then, from a casual remark made by his wife's visitor, he remembers, with pride and joy, that he is a chess-player. He knows he must hide this discovery, and when his former teacher Valentinov tries to contact him, Luzhin believes that a trap is being set for him. He can escape the trap only with an unexpected move; he escapes it by committing suicide.

Luzhin has a passion for order, and in fact can only understand an ordered universe. The order he perceives in the world outside chess is some other game, in which he is not a person but a pawn. As a child he knows that being an adult means he will, in others' eyes, lose his humanity. Going to school means that he will be called by his surname and this prospect makes him frantic. (It is only at the end of the novel, when he has thrown himself from the window, that the reader learns his Christian names.) Going to school means that his private order will be destroyed and he will be subject to others' order in which he is, as his fiancée's mother declares, 'not a person'. His talent for chess gains his father's approval, but not his love, and Luzhin's association with Valentinov enforces beyond reprieve his incapacity to function within the world outside chess. His teacher

was interested in Luzhin only inasmuch as he remained a freak, an odd phenomenon, somewhat deformed but enchanting, like a dachshund's crooked legs. During the whole time that he lived with Luzhin he unremittingly encouraged and developed his gift, not bothering for a second about Luzhin as a person, whom, it seemed, not only Valentinov but life itself had overlooked [. . . Luzhin] had become attached to Valentinov early [. . .] and later he regarded him the way a son might a frivolous, coldish, elusive father to whom one could never say how much one loved him. Valentinov was interested in him only as a chess player [. . .] The food he chose for him was light so that his brain could function freely, but for some reason [. . .] he encouraged Luzhin a great deal in his passion for sweets. Finally he had a peculiar theory that the development of Luzhin's gift for chess was connected with the development of the sexual urge, that with him chess represented a special deflection of this urge, and fearing lest Luzhin should squander his precious power in releasing by natural means the beneficial inner tension, he kept him at a distance from women and rejoiced over his chaste moroseness. There was something degrading in all this; Luzhin, recalling that time, was surprised to note that not a single, kind, humane word had ever passed between him and Valentinov.[11]

Luzhin's fragmented perceptions result from what others have taught him: others see only fragments of him, and he implicitly trusts them. It is as though he thinks, 'People are justified in their limited vision — that is how to look at things.' Yet when Luzhin does discover a complete person in the medley of his perceptions, he immediately falls in love. The young woman speaks to him and he initially confuses her with a prostitute he had met in another city:

This was his first impression when he saw her, when he noticed with surprise that he was actually talking to her. It irked him a little that she was not quite as good-looking as she might have been, judging by odd dreamy signs strewn about in his past. He reconciled himself to this and gradually began to forget her vague prototypes, and then he felt reassured and proud that here talking to him, spending her time with him and smiling at him, was a real live person.[12]

The woman is amused and touched by his helplessness, yet her genuine love and desire to help him are as destructive as everyone else's self-interest. She is sufficiently independent to defy her parents' notion of a 'good match' but not to doubt the validity of the doctor's proscription against chess. Luzhin's education has made him fit for nothing other than chess, but he is then deprived of chess. As he squeezes himself through the bathroom window the eternity that is 'obligingly and inexorably spread out before him' is a chasm divided, like a chessboard, into pale and dark squares.

Chess provides the order Luzhin craves and the only order he understands. It is the means by which he deals with reality — but, of course, it is no means of dealing with reality. The intrusions upon his carefully constructed order must be resisted. He runs away when his parents declare that he will now start school, for school will deprive him of the familiar patterns, the habitual walks and little luxuries that make up his day: 'In exchange for all this came something new, unknown and therefore hideous, an impossible, unacceptable world.'[13] The unknown is unacceptable, even unreal. It is during various domestic upheavals and plots that he learns chess, in contrast to which everything else is like a dream: 'Real life, chess life, was orderly, clear-cut, and rich in adventure, and Luzhin noted with pride how easy it was for him to reign in this life, and the way everything obeyed his will and bowed to his schemes.'[14]

Nevertheless, before his tournament with Turati, Luzhin can, just about, function with his piecemeal perceptions. He can travel, he can keep appointments, and he even manages to propose to the young woman:

'She's sure to be in her room,' he said as he went up the stairs. He burst in upon her as if he had butted the door with his head, and dimly catching sight of her reclining in a pink dress on the couch, he said hastily: 'H'llo — h'llo,' and strode all around the room, supposing that everything was working out very easily, wittily and entertaining-ly, and simultaneously suffocating with excitement. 'And therefore in continuance of the above I have to inform you that you will be my wife, I implore you to agree to this, it was absolutely impossible to go away, now everything will be different and wonderful,' and at this point he settled on a chair by the radiator and, covering his face with his hands, burst into tears; then trying to spread one hand so that it covered his face he began with the other to search for his handkerchief, and through the trembling wet chinks between his fingers he perceived in duplicate a blurry pink dress that noisily moved towards him. 'Now, now, that's enough, that's enough,' she repeated in a soothing voice. 'A grown man and crying like that.' He seized her by the elbow and kissed something hard and cold — her wristwatch. She removed his straw hat and stroked his forehead — and swiftly retreated, evading his clumsy, grabbing movements.[15]

This success in the sphere outside chess is paid for by a greater severity in chess's demands upon him:

Luzhin, preparing an attack for which it was first necessary to explore a maze of variations, where his every step aroused a perilous echo, began a long meditation [...] Suddenly, something occurred outside his being, a scorching pain — and he let out a long cry, shaking his hand stung by the flame of a match, which he had lit and forgotten to apply to his cigarette. The pain immediately passed, but in the fiery gap he had seen something unbearable awesome, the full horror of the abysmal depths of chess. He glanced at the chessboard and his brain wilted from hitherto unprecedented weariness. But the chessmen were pitiless, they held and absorbed him. There was horror in this, but in this was also the sole harmony, for what else exists in the world besides chess? Fog, the unknown, non-being [...][16]

The supreme reality of chess now makes the ordinary world unrecognisable, and Luzhin cannot find his way about even on the simplest level. He opens a door and expects to find the chess tournament in process, but instead sees a corridor he cannot traverse. When the chess game is over, he does not know how to get out of the room. In every corner he sees a chess attack developing; the people and furniture alike are chess figures. He is diagnosed as having a 'nervous breakdown', but what is actually happening is that he is losing his innocence; he is beginning to discover how the ordinary world runs itself.

Married, and deprived of chess, Luzhin is deprived of any purpose and any ability to master his life. Aware of his powerlessness, the world seems monstrous. He must 'contrive a defence against this perfidious combination' for he understands that people either want something of him, or try to keep him in a certain place, or move him in a certain way. He learns a few rules of the new game: he can 'glue together and sew up a smile' for his wife to disguise his knowledge that she is planning a new move, and he can keep the memory of his chess days a secret, but he cannot maintain control. When he finds a chess-set in the lining of an old jacket there is no place to hide his treasure: 'Everywhere was insecure. The most unexpected places were invaded in the mornings by the snout of that rapacious vacuum cleaner. It is difficult, difficult to hide a thing the other things are jealous and inhospitable, holding on firmly to their places and not allowing a homeless object, escaping pursuit, into a single cranny.'[17] Ordinary objects become part of the plot against him, and he has no reprieve.

Luzhin invents a toothache to explain his silence and low spirits, and the tender concern he arouses in his wife also forms part of the combination against him. He tells her that his only hope is to drop out of the game: 'Game? Are we going to play?' she asked tenderly, and simultaneously thought that she had to powder her face, the guests would be here any minute.'[18] She believes she is acting on Luzhin's behalf and therefore does not acknowledge her part in the game, but Luzhin, unaware of the rules of normal behaviour, is threatened by the moves he cannot understand. He cannot sleep because sleep 'consisted of sixty-four squares, a gigantic board in the middle of which, trembling and stark-naked, Luzhin stood, the size of a pawn, and peered at the dim positions of huge pieces, megacephalous, with crowns or manes.'[19] Events are broken up and then rejoined to take their places on the board: the photographer's hand moving Luzhin's head into position for his passport photo (the prospective journey, he is sure, is a decisive move) becomes the dentist's hand moving his jaw into position, and the stamp on the passport photo becomes the dentist's marks on the X-rays, all of which indicate a plan Luzhin cannot interpret. Even his escape from the game — his suicide — is a move within the game, however unexpected, and the ground towards which he hurtles is marked out like a chess-set.

Luzhin is not mad in the way in which Chekhov's Gromov in 'Ward Six' is, nor in the way that Gogol's diarist is mad. He sees, correctly, what is happening to him, and his condition could be diagnosed as paranoia only if the nature and needs of his self were denied legitimacy. He feels deprived of his dignity (for, despite the comic and even grotesque figure he cuts, Luzhin's sensitivity and capacity for concentration ensure his dignity) and, more importantly, of that single but exciting world which he can master. Luzhin is totally confused about anything outside chess, yet he is justified in applying certain aspects of chess to his 'real' life and in so doing highlights aspects of that reality which other people ignore: knowing the rules, they forget that they are acting according to rules, whereas Luzhin, ignorant of the rules, sees how fierce and threatening they can be. The ordinary world, to Luzhin, is fantastic, and his fantastic vision discloses the nature of the ordinary world.

Like most other fantasists Nabokov is intrigued by the double theme. *Despair* (1966) is his most popular treatment of that theme. It is a wonderfully suggestive novel, though unfortunately the suggestions are multiplied without being developed. There is a tantalizing link made between a search for the double and a death-wish: Hermann sees the sleeping tramp as a perfect replica of his corpse, and he is disappointed by the signs of life, which mar the resemblance. Hermann's aim in using the man he believes to be his double is to murder his respectable self (the plot to get the insurance money is merely an excuse) and take on the character of a dirty and outcast self. He is proud of his ingenuity and secrecy, yet he proves himself to be totally naïve about others' secrecy. (Any reasonable person would see proof that his wife is having an affair with her cousin when he finds them alone, undressed, lying in bed, but Hermann unreflectingly accepts their explanations.) He is proud, too, of his ability to disguise his handwriting (an ability he greatly over-estimates) yet he is plagued by nightmares of perpetual counterfeits. He is sexually excited by the idea of splitting himself: as he makes love to his wife he imagines that he is watching himself make love to her, and the further away he can imagine himself to be from the bed, the more arousing he finds the proceedings. These variations on the double theme, however, are sacrificed to Nabokov's clever story. At the close of the novel, Hermann is simply a criminal on the run, having failed to remove a crucial clue from his abandoned car, and having grossly over-estimated his ability to present and manipulate illusions.

The Eye (1966) is a more simple but also more successful double story. The narrator is attacked by a jealous husband and believes himself to be dead: the doctor's announcement that the bullet went straight through him without injuring the lung is, he believes, a hallucination. Dead himself, he now follows the fortunes of Smirnov, a totally unremarkable, even abject figure who, to impress an attractive woman, relates stories in which he is an endangered hero, the falsehood of which is obvious to everyone but the narrator — and thus is it clear that the narrator is

Smirnov. When the narrator himself realises this, he is disappointed: his conviction that everything was a dream provided him with a splendid irresponsibility — that of being without a central self, for

> the only happiness in this world is to observe, to spy, to watch, to scrutinise oneself and others, to be nothing but a big, vitreous, somewhat bloodshot, unblinking eye [...] What does it matter that I am a bit cheap, a bit foul, and that no one appreciated all the remarkable things about me [...] The world, try as it may, cannot insult me. I am invulnerable.[20]

The Eye thus presents the distinction between a person as a sentient actor and as an observer of his own thoughts, feelings and actions as a splitting into two people. The self as observer is not (as is Freud's super-ego) a critical observer, but rather like the audience of a play with a special fondness for or lenience towards one character. In psychoanalytic theory identification with the self as observer indicates a heightening of critical (or moral) feeling, but Nabokov presents a possibility in which the identification abrogates responsibility and judgement. Observation serves as a defence against criticism and involvement. Even before one's own fantasies one is passive. As in 'The Visit to the Museum' Nabokov challenges the cliché that one is responsible for one's fantasies or dreams, though here he does not offer merely a paradoxical denial, but a plausible case. Smirnov's defence is certainly paltry and cowardly — not because he abrogates responsibilities for his fantasies but because he evades responsibility for his actions. The transformation fantasy which is the counterpart to this abrogation (he is only an eye, much as David Alan Kepesh is only one enormous breast) obliterates the self; the person is not a double self, and his capacity for self-observation is not an indication of an independent authority.

Like *Despair*, *The Eye* is constructed in the form of a detective story. The puzzling sequence of events can essentially be explained in terms of the narrator's mad self-aggrandisement. Plentiful clues as to the quality of the narrator's confusions are dispersed throughout the novel, and thus the author's wry logic keeps the fantasy elements within the scope of realism.

The tale 'Lik' (1939), now published in *Nabokov's Quartet*, however, does not use simple misapprehension to perpetrate confusion, and it is Nabokov's finest and most subtle use of the double theme. This brief story is set in a small town on the French Mediterranean during the 1930s. A young man in his thirties, a Russian expatriate and orphan, is a member of an actors' touring company. In the play presented he appears as a Russian who inspires love in both a mother and daughter. The character, though crucial to the drama, cuts an insignificant figure on the stage, and has very few lines. Lik, who has a weak heart and knows that he will soon die, must handle himself carefully in the hot climate, and spends most of his time between performances resting. By chance he meets Koldunov, an old schoolmate and distant relative, who persuades him to accompany him home and to drink wine, disastrous to his health. Lik manages to escape and to resist Koldunov's pleas for a loan, but he realises he has left behind the package containing a pair of shoes he has just bought. Calculating that he has enough time to return to his cousin's flat before his performance, he goes back to collect the package. As he arrives he hears a shot. Koldunov has just killed himself, and on his feet are Lik's new white shoes.

The appropriation of Lik's shoes does not imply that Lik has, or has not, adequately put himself in his cousin's position, or that he should, morally speaking, imagine himself to be his cousin. Rather, the new white shoes on the dead man's feet, underlining his macabre squalor (even as his despair is suicidal, he must steal whatever he can), offer a startling and awful explanation of Lik's susceptibility to Koldunov's bullying: Koldunov is Lik's true self, against which he has been protected by his superficiality.

Lik — which means 'appearance' both in Russian and Middle English — cannot value actuality more than possibility. It is unclear whether he

possessed genuine theatrical talent or was a man of many indistinct callings who had chosen one of them at random but could just as well have been a painter, jeweller, or rat-catcher. Such a person resembles a room with a number of different doors, among which there is perhaps one that does lead straight into some great garden, into the moonlit depths of a marvellous human night, where the soul discovers the treasure intended for it alone. But, be that as it may, Lik had failed to open *that* door, taking instead the Thespian path, which he followed without enthusiasm, with the absent manner of a man looking for signposts that do not exist but that perhaps have appeared to him in a dream, or can be distinguished in the undeveloped photograph of some other locality that he will never, never visit.[21]

Deprived of parents, his country and — because of his heart condition — life itself, he has no self-identifying attachments. Thus, whatever he happens to be, is inconsequential; whatever position he may actually have has no impact upon him. He joined the acting company as casually 'as a fur doffed by a woman lands on this or that quite anonymous chair'. He remains a stranger within the company, and always feels superfluous, or as though he has usurped someone else's place. If his colleagues are friendly, he interprets their behaviour as indifference, or supposes that they have made a mistake and mean to address someone else.

Lik's disregard for the actual leads to the clumsiness commonly described in fantasy literature: he cannot take care of physical objects even if he should happen to value them. His deficiencies compel him, as his only hope, to believe in the reality and glamour of the theatre. The only words he exchanges with the leading lady are the lines they speak on stage, and he likes to tell himself that only there does she lead her real life, 'being subject the rest of the time to periodic fits of insanity, during which she no longer recognised him and called herself by a different name'.[22] Since the normal processes of life present him with no identity or significance, he hopes that he will die on stage, and in dying discover the play to be his new reality, for 'if death did not present him with an exit into true reality, he would simply never come to know life.'[23]

Lik's affinity with the typical Romantic impasse makes him susceptible not to ecstatic or mystical-sensuous visions, but to ponderous and tawdry nightmares, the basis of which is his impotence, that is, his belief that any choice he makes will be ineffectual. Therefore he has no reason to make decisions. With no influence on the direction and course of his life, he is particularly sensitive to Koldunov's bullying. Lik had supposed his childhood tormentor to be dead, yet dreams

would still occur even now, for there was no control over them. Sometimes Koldunov would appear in person, in his own image, in the surroundings of boyhood, hastily assembled by the director of dreams out of such accessories as a classroom, desks, a blackboard, and its dry, weightless sponge. Besides these down-to-earth dreams there were also romantic even decadent ones — devoid, that is, of Koldunov's obvious presence but coded by him, saturated with his oppressive spirit or filled with rumours about him, with situations and shadows of situations somehow expressing his essence.[24]

The Koldunov he meets as an adult is no longer much larger than Lik, nor can he command the schoolboy audience that would encourage his abuse. Koldunov is now a true 'loser', filching money and cigarettes, pleading for a loan, certain to be refused. His plight evinces revulsion rather than sympathy, and he seems to delight in exhibiting his poverty

and failure. Imagining Lik to be successful, he is confirmed in his belief
that the world is against him:

> 'What went wrong? No, you tell *me* — what went wrong? I just
> want to know what went wrong, then I'll be satisfied. Why has life
> systematically baited me? Why have I been assigned the part of some
> miserable scoundrel who is spat on by everybody, gypped, bullied,
> thrown into jail? [...] You go swaggering around, living in hotels,
> smooching with actresses [...] What's the reason for it? Come on,
> explain it to me.'
>   Lik said, 'I turned out to have — I happen to have ... Oh, I don't
> know ... a modest dramatic talent, I suppose you could say.'
>   'Talent?' shouted Koldunov. 'I'll show you talent! [...] So,
> according to you, I'm the lowest, filthiest vermin and deserve my
> rotten end?'[25]

Koldunov reasons that if Lik believes his success has an explanation, then
he must also believe that Koldunov's failure has an explanation: if Lik
explains his success in terms of talent, then Koldunov's failure is due to
lack of talent. Though Koldunov's logic is paranoidal, it mirrors Lik's
conviction that he ought to have been someone else. Koldunov believes
he ought to have been Lik; Lik's idea is too vague to resist the implication
that he ought to have been Koldunov.

Lik is affected by Koldunov as by a double. The pressure his cousin
exerts upon him is such that Lik expects his weak heart to give way. Yet
even when he manages to escape he decides to return to Koldunov, to
make the claim, 'Those are mine,' of the dead man's shoes. The
compulsion to assert the identity is stronger even than the revulsion and
defeat he feels in Koldunov's presence. Their meeting is certainly a
harbinger of death. The surprise is that Koldunov dies first. Thus it
appears that Lik has unwittingly acted as Koldunov's double. The
superficial realism of the tale allows Nabokov to present the double in a
reciprocal relationship — and he is the only fantasist who does this
successfully. (Hoffmann, in *The Devil's Elixirs*, shows a reciprocal double
relationship between Brother Medardus and Count Victor, but the
characters are too fragmented to be identifiable as personalities, and thus
the reciprocity has no psychological point.) The fact that each character is
an ordinary human being, without special powers of knowledge or
mobility, means that each is plagued in his idiosyncratic way by fear and
despair in confrontation with the other. For Koldunov, Lik is the
fortunate person he ought to have been, from whom he is therefore

entitled to take everything; so that when Koldunov fails to extract anything significant from Lik, he commits suicide. Lik's aversion to Koldunov makes him highly vulnerable to his cousin's influence; he is suffocated by Koldunov's intimacy and abusiveness, and fears that he will die within this awful trap, excluded from the releasing death he hopes to find on stage. This sound psychological story with its realistic settings discloses the fantastic dimensions of normal responses.

7 Logical Fantasy: Jorge Luis Borges

Fantasy in modern literature depends upon realism in literature: it depends upon the reader's ability to recognise a commonly acknowledged, or normal, world and to recognise descriptions as pertaining to, or failing to pertain to, normal conditions. The initial impact of fantasy is its deviation from the norm. The further and more fascinating impact of fantasy arises from its connections to the norm, from the way in which it highlights the instability, inconsistency or underlying preposterousness of the normal. Jorge Luis Borges uses fantasy not only to challenge assumptions about the normal world but also to challenge conventional descriptions of it. He is a literatary metaphysician, investigating logic through fantasy.

Metaphysics, at its most respectable, is the attempt to present the logical structure of the universe. It is therefore intimately connected to the question of how we come to know the world and how it can be known. Knowledge of the world is a function of its logical structure, whether it is supposed that we give it that structure, or whether it has that structure independently of human perception. The purpose of metaphysics is to analyse fundamental concepts of knowledge, including cause and effect, physical reality and mental phenomena. Metaphysics analyses; it does not prescribe or proscribe. Nevertheless it has the habit of making the commonplace appear very strange. In describing the world we all know so well it seems to transform it into a confusing and foreign place. Thus Bishop Berkeley, in describing the relation between perceptions and physical objects, declares that there is an unbridgeable gap between what we see and what there is in the world if we suppose that there is something 'behind' or independent of what we see. He therefore denies (and commonsense would support his denial) that there is a bridge between what we perceive and what exists, and then concludes, in defiance of commonsense, that what exists is constituted by our perceptions. The usual belief that we see things is replaced by the theory that we

111

see our perceptions, which are things, and the theory is supported by the simple truth that we come to know the world only by our perceptions of the world. Berkeley had, as Hume noted, constructed a model of perception and reality that was both ridiculous and irrefutable.

On these grounds alone Berkeley's theory would be ruled out by some philosophers: if it cannot be refuted then nothing would be different if it were not the case, and therefore it is an empty proposition — or indeed a non-proposition. The theory nevertheless presents an intriguing picture — a perfect example of the sort of thing that intrigue Borges, for it seems to be constructed with impeccable logic yet at the same time it defies ordinary logic. Borges is fascinated by order, by the order we ourselves are compelled to construct. His fantasies make use of this compulsion and underline the way in which logic serves, not dispels, fantasy.

In 'Tlön, Uqbar, Orbis Tertius', from *Fictions* (1956), Borges describes a world in which Berkeley's theory would not be strange. The nations of the planet of Tlön are congenitally idealist; their language and all its derivatives — their literature, religion and metaphysics — presuppose idealism. Thus the people of Tlön do not believe the world to be a concurrence of objects in space, but a heterogeneous series of independent acts; their world is serial and temporal, but not spatial.

Borges's story draws the implications of Berkeley's thesis. If objects are equivalent to perceptions, then there is no space, for space involves motion in and among physical objects — space is defined by the arrangement of physical objects. According to Berkeley the various angles and arrangements and degrees of distinctness of objects — which we normally take to be clues about the objects' position in space — merely form part of a predictable visual series: from the present appearance of an object we can expect other appearances if we move (though the notion of our movement, too, must be modified) this way or that.

Idealism also throws out the ordinary belief that objects are independent of perceptions and exist while they are not being perceived. Thus we can no longer postulate that the desk we are sitting at today is the same as the desk at which we were sitting yesterday, for if we cannot suppose that the desk endured while we were not perceiving it, yesterday's desk and today's desk cannot be assumed to be identical. In fact, in Tlön the question of a physical object's identity over a period of time is as nonsensical as the question about the identity of two pains suffered at different times. To attribute identity on the basis of exact similarity (e.g., some coins are lost along a road at one time and some coins, similar to those lost, are found at a later time: they are therefore assumed, in a non-idealist world, to be identical) is as absurd as to suppose that nine similar coins are also one coin.

Borges describes how Tlön adapts to the implications of idealism: cause and effect are interpreted as the association of ideas; tactual and visual systems are separate, unbound by the notion of an external object being perceived in different ways. Thus far Borges is merely covering the ground of the philosopher, but he extends his scope when first he explains that in Tlön metaphysicians are not seeking truth, or even an approximation of truth; rather, they are seeking a kind of amazement. Metaphysics is a branch of fantastic literature: 'They know that a system is nothing more than a subordination of all the aspects of the universe to some one of them.'[1] Yet this knowledge does not lessen the implications of their metaphysical beliefs, which change the face of reality. Perception is always selective, and in Tlön the selection is carried out on behalf of the prevailing metaphysics. Borges suggests effects of such selection: objects perceived which are especially close to expectations of perceptions form a distinct class of objects called *hrönir,* and since satisfied expectations lead to other expectations, there are complicated degrees of *hrönir,* each degree varying in purity of form. Objects, too, can be brought into being by hope, and since they have a special link with ideas they can also be lost or effaced or fragmented by forgetfullness.

The metaphysics of Tlön satisfies the intellect's craving for order, and because it is a constructed order, rather than one supposed to be true, it can be constructed with complete consistency, as a 'true' order never is, or never is perceived to be:

Ten years ago, any symmetrical system whatsoever which gave the appearance of order — dialectical materialism, anti-Semitism, Nazism — was enough to fascinate men. Why not fall under the spell of Tlön and submit to the minute and vast evidence of an ordered planet? Useless to reply that reality, too, is ordered. It may be so, but in accord with divine laws — I translate: inhuman laws — which we will never completely perceive. Tlön may be a labyrinth, but it is a labyrinth plotted by men, a labyrinth destined to be deciphered by men.[2]

Thus, while Borges mocks idealism, showing how it does not apply to our world, he at the same time justifies it as a psychological exercise: our intellect is such that it must create orders.

The tension between the need to believe in order and, in reality, either the absence of order or man's lack of power to perceive reality's order, may lead not only to confusion but to cruelty. Thus in 'Deutsches Requiem', from *The Aleph* (1947), the Nazi-narrator's antagonist is a Jewish poet who 'takes joy in each thing, with a scrupulous, exact love', never cataloguing or enumerating, content with pure individuality. The Nazi, a sub-director of a concentration camp, drives the poet mad by hounding him with the unwieldliness of particularity: 'I had come to understand many years before that there is nothing on earth that does not contain the seed of a possible Hell; a face, a word, a compass, a cigarette advertisement, are capable of driving a person mad if he is unable to forget them.'[3] His aim in destroying the poet is to destroy a detested zone of his own soul. The Nazi's craving for order is such that his punishment, after Germany's defeat, is acceptable as part of a wide view of order: 'Many things will have to be destroyed in order to construct the New Order; now we know that Germany also was one of those things [...] Let Heaven exist, even though our dwelling place is Hell.'[4] Order is his only morality. The narrator accepts the view that Nazism was evil only because it disintegrated into chaos. Thus does Borges combine apt comments upon the psychology of the historical phenomenon of Nazism with a more general point about the psychology of logic.

In 'The Mirror of Enigmas'[5] Borges offers an example of divine intelligence: the steps a man takes, from his birth to his death, trace a figure in time, inconceivable to man, but as clear to the divine intelligence as the figure of a triangle is to man; it is a figure which, moreover, may have its determined function in the economy of the universe. The divine construction is as fantastic as Tlön's metaphysics, but it is supremely consistent.

Borges, like Poe and Dürrenmatt, sees the detective story as a complement to the fantasy tale: the former shows how the grotesque and confusing form of the latter can be mastered; the detective's intelligence, like the divine intelligence, traces a logical figure within wilfully perpetrated confusions. 'The Garden of Forking Paths' (*Fictions*) links the detective's intellect with the writer's discipline. A fiction draws a single figure within a maze of possibilities. Every event in fiction presents the author with a new set of possibilities from which he must choose. Thus the commonplace belief that the writer is circumscribed by his 'knowledge' of the characters is unmasked by the logic of the writer's enterprise. 'The Garden of Forking Paths' describes a Chinese novel in which the author has refused to limit the story so severely and thus has outlined all possible solutions to each event. Since one future rules out another, this novel, which outlines many possible futures, is full of contradictions, and yet remains true to the logic of fiction.

The author of the labyrinthine novel is an ancestor of the protagonist spy, who discusses the book with a well-known Sinologist. During the discussion, a man comes in the garden in pursuit of the spy. Suddenly, instead of trying to flee, the spy shoots the Sinologist. The spy's task was to convey to his country's enemies the name of the city that is to be attacked — the city is Albert, and the name of the Sinologist he shot was Stephen Albert. The news of the murder will reach his chief, and will adequately convey his message.

The criminal's usual task is to hide the actual figure of events, but here the spy's task is to construct a figure to be read by his chief, but to be ignored by everyone else. The most puzzling aspect of this story, however, is the point at which the spy decided to draw this particular figure. It is possible that his plan had been formed as soon as he disembarked from the train, but it is also possible that he constructed this possibility from fortuitous occurrences. For when he was at the station some children asked him (presumably because he was Chinese) whether he was going to visit the Sinologist Stephen Albert; his plan could have been formed then, or even later, when he knew his pursuer was approaching him from the garden path.

Borges also considers the supposition, based upon the coherence theory of truth, that any one statement, or even a single word, if perfectly understood, would reveal every truth. In 'The God's Script'[6] a prisoner imagines a language which would be disclosed in the configuraton of the tiger's spots:

> I considered that even in the human languages there is no proposition that does not imply the entire universe [...] I considered that in the language of a god every word would enunciate that infinite concatenation of facts, and not in an implicit but in an explicit manner, and not progressively but instantaneously. In time, the notion of a divine sentence seemed puerile or even blasphemous. A god, I reflected, ought to utter only a single word and in that word absolute fullness.[7]

The prisoner's philosophy of language is similar to that of the idealist F.H. Bradley, who believed that the truth of any one statement rests upon the truth of all statements and that the complete class of true statements can in principle be derived from any one true statement; for that statement is true which coheres with all other true statements, and the coherence is such that all true statements can be read off from any single true statement. In 'The God's Script' Borges extends this notion, implausibly, to a single word. Frequently Borges writes about the power of a single word or phrase. In 'The Mirror and the Mask' from *The Book of Sand* (1975) the essence of beauty is expressed in a single line of poetry; the poet must kill himself and the king who learned the magical line is condemned to become a wanderer. In 'Undr', also from *The Book of Sand*, the chosen word is widely known but rarely understood, and its understanding brings peace rather than despair. Borges's satisfying, teasing logic is absent from these tales, which make use of magical themes without indicating possible, paradoxical truths. Only in 'The Aleph' does he elaborate upon the possibility of a minute but all-encompassing image; and here he avoids confusions about the nature of language, for the Aleph is an object, not a term or phrase or sentence. It is a sphere of intolerable brilliance which is the sum of all possible visual representations — a claim which commands reverence, but which is also untestable and which thereby indicates the status and aim of religious claims.

Alongside the presentation of infinite concentration and conciseness Borges investigates the possibility of a breakdown in classification and representation — the possibility that plagued the Nazi narrator of 'Deutsches Requiem'. 'Funes, the Memorius'[8] describes the mind of an uneducated young man who, after a head injury, develops total recall. The remarkable capacity creates an impasse: his memory of his past life is tantamount to a re-living of his life, and at the same time he must remember himself remembering his life. Perfect memory locks him in eternal remembering. Yet the paradox fails to bite, because Borges's model of what it is to remember is crude and confused. To remember is not to re-live, and having a perfect memory would be having the ability to recall everything, not engaging in the process of remembering everything. A similar confusion is made in Borges's puzzle about the perfect map: it would be co-extensive with the terrain it represents, and thus would require the same space. The point made is too simplistic to be strange or exciting. A map represents or records, and a 'perfect' map is also a useful one, and therefore not co-extensive with the terrain it represents. The need for order and representation may lead us astray, but certain representations are not puzzling.

What Borges emphasises, however, is the fascination of the particular, a fascination he himself creates to reveal the terrifying possibility of the breakdown in our ability to classify, which would also be a breakdown of balance and sanity. In 'The Zahir' (from *Fictions*) the narrator, after attending a wake for a woman who continually searched for perfection of disdain, snobbery and breeding, goes into a bar where three men are playing cards — a game of chance which is in marked contradiction to the Absolute which, the narrator believes, the woman had achieved in death. He receives, in his change from the purchase of a drink, a Zahir, a coin worth twenty centavos. In Arabic 'Zahir' means 'notorious', 'visible'. It is one of the ninety-nine names of God, and people in Muslim territories use it to signify 'beings or things which possess the terrible property of being unforgettable, and whose image finally drives one mad'. The coin, handed to the narrator quite fortuitously, apparently in contradiction to the absolute face of death he has previously witnessed, itself becomes an absolute. It forms the centre of his consciousness, though for a while the periphery of consciousness is still alive, and he can forget the Zahir by composing fantasies — these engage his attention more than reality; subsequently he can avoid the Zahir by contemplating its opposite, but soon even the opposite of the Zahir has the Zahir in its centre. Various possibilities arise from this compulsion: according to idealist tenets, if all men dream about the Zahir and see the Zahir everywhere, then the Zahir will become the sole reality; or, it is possible that his repeated contemplation of the Zahir will wear it away, as though his thoughts were like water upon stone, and then, behind the Zahir, he will find God.

The Zahir is not a symbol. Its fascination stems from a concreteness that dominates consciousness without having allusive power, and therefore deadens as it dominates. 'The Zahir' presents both a comic and awful vision of absolutely meaningless obsession.

In 'The Disk' and 'The Book of Sand' — both from *The Book of Sand* — Borges describes similar instances of obssession with objects, though in these tales the objects described become obssessions because they are impossible constructions. The disk is a one-sided object only, with the fairy-tale property of making the owner a king. The woodcutter kills the man who holds it, but as the man falls, the disk falls so that the side it lacks is the side that is facing upwards, and therefore it will never be found. The book of sand has an infinite number of pages, neatly contained in a single, manageable volume. Thus the reader can get hopelessly lost in the text, and at the same time can expect endless adventures. The narrator who discovers the special properties of the book guards against the obsession which destroys the owner of the Zahir and loses the volume amid the shelves of a vast library. The human intellect may crave order, but in a world of particular objects it may get hopelessly stuck on one fascinating particular, especially if it defies the known order. The craving for order can be seen as a defence against this fascination.

Borges insists that order is a fantasy, but at the same time order rules our lives as though it were a natural law. 'The Babylon Lottery'[9] presents a mirror to commonplace explanations of occurrences, though the image reflected seems outlandish. The narrator comes from a country in which a lottery determines a wide range of events. For most of his life he has unquestioningly accepted the function of the lottery; only in leaving his country has he become aware of the peculiarity of his assumptions. What happened in Babylon is this: a lottery gradually developed by which the life, death and position of the inhabitants were decided; the lottery grew more powerful and more specific, determining not only life, death and position, but the circumstances of the individual's lives and the manner of their deaths, for

> if the lottery is an intensification of chance, a periodic infusion of chaos into the cosmos, would it not be desirable for chance to intervene at all stages of the lottery and not merely in the drawing? Is it not ridiculous for chance to dictate the death of someone, while the circumstances of his death — its silent reserve or publicity, the time limit of one hour or one century — should remain immune to hazard? These eminently just scruples finally provoked a considerable reform [. . .][10]

The Company which runs the lottery is shrouded in mystery. Some declare the Company to be eternal, some declare that it never existed and never will, and some declare that the question of the Company's existence is unimportant, since things would proceed in the same way whether or not the Company existed. Thus the argument of the Company's existence forms an analogy to familiar arguments about God's existence, just as the tightening control of the lottery is analogous to a growing belief in determinism. The lottery, which originated from the desire to introduce chaos into order, became accepted as the norm and therefore the lottery was conceived as a regulator of order.

The futile search for order, the belief in a divine order alongside the construction of a pedestrian and meaningless order are elements to be found in Kafka's *The Castle*, but Borges's use of them in 'The Library of Babel'[11] emphasises the logical weight against a successful search, rather than the psychological defeat. The Library is, or is thought to be, co-extensive with the universe, though it is ordered in a way we do not suppose our universe to be; it is composed of 'an indefinite, perhaps an infinite, number of hexagonal galleries, with enormous ventilation shafts in the middle, encircled by very low railings'.[12] The fact that all galleries are thus shaped leads the idealists to argue that the hexagonal halls are realisations of the only possible form, that any other spacial form is inconceivable. The Library is seen as a work of God, partaking of divine order and eternity, though the inhabitants' lives may be merely fortuitous. The scripts in the Library are divine, and since they contain all possible combinations of orthographic symbols, a volume, somewhere, contains the answers to all questions of the meaning and purpose of individual existence:

> When it was proclaimed that the Library comprised all books, the first impression was one of extravagant joy. All men felt themselves lords of a secret, intact treasure. There was no personal or universal problem whose eloquent solution did not exist — in some hexagon. The universe was justified, the universe suddenly expanded to the limitless dimensions of hope. At that time there was much talk of the Vindications: books of apology and prophecy, which vindicated for all time the actions of every man in the world and established a store of prodigious arcana for the future. Thousands of covetous persons abandoned their dear natal hexagons and crowded up the stairs, urged on by the vain aim of finding their Vindication. These pilgrims disputed in the narrow corridors, hurled dark maledictions, strangled each other on the divine stairways, flung the deceitful books to the bottom of the tunnels, and died as they were thrown into space by men from remote regions. Some went mad [. . .]
> The Vindications do exist. I have myself seen two of these books, which were concerned with future people, people who were perhaps not imaginary. But the searchers did not remember that the calculable possibility of a man's finding his own book, or some perfidious variation of his own book, is close to zero.[13]

Borges's model of the search for understanding is indeed frightening: there is no gradual building up of knowledge, no careful extension of vision; there is only a search against all odds for a vindication of a life which seems, from Borges's laconic description, deadly. Indeed, whereas Kafka's tales of lives wasted by search and hope cannot actually be read as parables, since the compulsion to search is beyond reason, Borges's tales could be construed as parables: he argues against the search for divine order and offers in consolation the intellectual satisfaction of creating bizarre but comprehensible orders.

The systems his tales depict are not always cosmic. The individual, dealing with personal concerns, must also create an order which defines his goals or protects him against his fears. Borges has been described as a non-psychological writer, eshewing psychology because its laws are too lax, embracing instead the construction of fictions in which everything has a perfectly logical place[14]; but Borges's fascination with logic reflects and comments upon the psychological compulsion to create a logical framework. 'Emma Zunz'[15] is the story of a construction of a fiction as the only means of dealing with a reality that becomes intolerable through disorder. The intolerable event is the suicide of Emma's father. He had been accused of embezzlement and had emigrated to Brazil, while she continued to work at the textile mill, now owned by Aaron Lowenthal who, her father believes, was the actual thief. When Emma learns of her father's suicide she, pretending to be an informer about industrial relations, has a private meeting with Lowenthal. Beforehand she had prostituted herself to a sailor, thus making her subsequent accusation that Lowenthal raped her, and that she shot him in revenge and defence, plausible. As she shoots Lowenthal, she discovers she is not avenging her father's death, but her dishonour by the sailor. Her story is believed because its emotional basis — the shame, hatred, outrage — are true; only the circumstances are false, and one or two proper names.

The concluding paradox — that Emma's story is true even though she falsifies those elements of the story which are ordinarily considered to be crucial to the truth of an accusation — does not carry much weight. After all, Lowenthal was guilty of the theft and therefore, however indirectly, morally responsible for her father's death, so that Borges's wry contradiction would not shock anyone's sensibilities, as it would if Emma's accusations were directed against someone who had no part in her father's history. What is of interest in the tale is the way Emma deals with a plot against her father by creating her own plot: fiction becomes a means of mastering the situation, both practically and psychologically. Borges describes the domination of the father's death with remarkable clarity, outlining the awful logic of a trauma:

> Emma dropped the paper. Her first impression was of a weak feeling in her stomach and in her knees; then of blind guilt, of unreality, of coldness, of fear; then she wished it were already the next day. Immediately afterwards she realised that that wish was futile because the death of her father was the only thing that had happened in the world, and that it would go on happening endlessly.[16]

The central fact is timeless and absolute, and all significant thoughts and actions must be related to it. She herself is subject to the importance of the central fact, and therefore her actions are more properly described as being decided by the plot, which is the solution to the trauma, than by herself: 'She picked up the piece of paper and went to her room. Furtively, she hid it in a drawer, as if somehow she already knew the ulterior facts. She had already begun to suspect them, perhaps; she had already become the person she would be.'[17] For she is now only a character in the plot.

Emma Zunz's reasoning, which makes her story credible, follows the dream reasoning Freud describes in his *The Interpretation of Dreams*. 'Therefore' and 'because' are terms involving logical thought which can be expressed by the manifest dream only in the primitive fashion of time sequence. Emma's dishonour with the sailor preceded her killing of Lowenthal, and therefore, if the events were to be interpreted as a manifest dream, the sequence would indicate a logical relation between the two events: she kills Lowenthal because she has been dishonoured by the sailor. Yet there is also an explanation well within the borders of ordinary logic: Emma prostitutes herself with the sailor as part of her plot to kill Lowenthal with impunity; and since Lowenthal is responsible — in her view — for her father's death, and since his death demands revenge, which is the aim of the plot, Lowenthal can be blamed for her sexual dishonour. The main point of her last-minute transformation of motive in killing Lowenthal, however, is that her plot has become her only truth, and that deception, which was its aim, has been superseded by her total subjection to the (almost involuntarily formed) story. Her terrible single-mindedness can be seen in the description of the murder:

> She squeezed the trigger twice. The large body collapsed as if the reports and the smoke had shattered it, the glass of water smashed, the face looked at her with amazement and anger, the mouth of the face swore at her in Spanish and Yiddish. The evil words did not slacken; Emma had to fire again. In the patio the chained dog broke out barking, and a gush of rude blood flowed from the obscene lips and soiled the beard and the clothing. Emma began the accusation she had prepared ('I have avenged my father and they will not be able to punish me ...') but she did not finish it, because Mr Lowenthal had already died. She never knew if he managed to understand.[18]

Emma looks upon her victim as she looks upon herself — as a character defined by his function in the story. She sees clearly all that is happening, but does not view it with human sympathies or fears. Her only interest, other than to kill Lowenthal, is to make him appreciate her motive, and therefore to understand his role in her fiction.

Emma uses a rigorously constructed fiction to guide her reality. The protagonist of 'The Waiting'[19] uses a fiction to abolish the force of reality. Knowing he will be killed, he imagines the moment of his death so many times that his actual death becomes, for him, part of yet another dream.

The story is that of a man in hiding who knows that eventually he will be found and killed. As he enters his new lodging the description of the room appears to be straightforward, even pedestrian, but in it we can see the man's anxiety to control his environment:

> Led by the woman, he crossed the entrance hall and the first patio. The room they had reserved for him opened, happily, on to the second patio. The bed was of iron, deformed by the craftsman into fantastic curves representing branches and tendrils; there was also a tall pine wardrobe, a bedside table, a shelf with books at floor level, two odd chairs and a washstand with its basin, jar, soap dish and bottle of turbid glass.[20]

This is not a competent spy gauging possible attacks and possible escape routes. It is the observation of someone who faces attacks from even self-created horrors and who has cause to worry about the grotesque suggestiveness of the bedstead: the observer is closer to Joseph K. than to 007. Since anyone might be his enemy, and since he is essentially powerless to combat his enemy, he must appease everyone, and at the same time must hide his anxiety to please:

> From his seat, the cabman returned one of the coins to him, a Uruguayan twenty-centavo piece which had been in his pocket since that night in the hotel at Melo. The man gave him forty centavos and immediately felt: 'I must act so that everyone will forgive me. I have made two errors: I have used a foreign coin and I have shown that the mistake matters to me.'[21]

Just as Emma Zunz became merely a character in her avenging plot, the man in 'The Waiting' is nothing other than the hunted man. If he were to discover that his pursuer is dead — and as a hunted man he must search the obituary columns in the hope of learning of his death — he would be utterly confused at having that fear, which is the basis of his life, dissipated. He even assumes the identity of his pursuer, using his name 'because it was impossible for him to think of any other'. He is protected from the normal run of nightmares by the dominating fear of his pursuer, and every dawn he dreams that he is being killed. One morning the hunters actually do find him:

> With a gesture, he asked them to wait and turned his face to the wall, as if to resume his sleep. Did he do it to arouse the pity of those who killed him, or because it is less difficult to endure a frightful happening than to imagine it and endlessly await it, or — and this is perhaps most likely — so that the murderers would be a dream, as they had already been so many times, in the same place, at the same hour?
> He was in this act of magic when the blast obliterated him. [22]

'The Waiting', like 'Emma Zunz', investigates the possible use of embracing and elaborating fiction as though it were reality — in other words, these tales investigate psychological uses of fantasy. Freud noted the repetition compulsion at work in the attempt to master traumatic events, and Borges extends Freud's description by showing how the repeated return to a feared occurrence (which in 'The Waiting' is future rather than past) masters the event or emotion not by realistic preparation but by allowing reality to take on the guise of a familiar fantasy. Thus the man's fantasy permits him to accept the reality of his imminent death though it is powerless to deflect it.

A similar theme can be seen in 'The Secret Miracle'. Like William Golding's *Pincher Martin* it describes an extended fantasy in the moment preceding death, but, despite its brevity, Borges's tale is far more complex than Golding's novel. The personal triumph Borges's Jaromir Hladik attains in his fantasy is not Pincher Martin's struggling survival, but a personal order that defies the political madness around him. Hladik dreams that he is partaking in a long-drawn-out chess game in which the contestants are two illustrious families and he, as the first born, must be a contender:

> The hour for the next move, which could not be postponed, struck on all the clocks. The dreamer ran across the sands of a rainy desert — and he could not remember the chessmen or the rules of chess. At this point he awoke. The din of the rain and the clangor of the terrible clocks ceased. A measured unison, sundered by voices of command, arose from the Zelternergasse. Day had dawned, and the armoured vanguards of the Third Reich were entering Prague. [23]

Hladik himself is at the mercy of an unknown and awful and ridiculous order. 'Two or three adjectives in Gothic script' suffice to convince the Gestapo of Hladik's pre-eminence and of the need for his death. As in 'The Waiting' anticipation of his death in the form of repeated imaginings of it are Hladik's means of 'mastering' it, though in this case he believes his imagination will have a negative effect upon reality:

> He infinitely anticipated the process, from the sleepless dawn to the mysterious discharge of rifles. Before the day set by Julius Rothe, he died hundreds of deaths [...] Then he would reflect that reality does not tend to coincide with forecasts about it. With perverse logic he inferred that to foresee a circumstantial detail is to prevent its happening. Faithful to this feeble magic, he would invent, *so that they might not happen,* the most atrocious particulars.[24]

Like Anton Petrovich in 'An Affair of Honour' Hladik uses the knowledge that his thoughts and desires are ineffectual to sneak in the hypothesis that he can control events, on the grounds that his expectations are bound to be false.

Hladik's fears gradually turn their focus away from death, which he cannot avoid, to the prospect of leaving his verse play unfinished. From this regret his imagination is able to save him. For, as Hladik faces the firing squad, he sees everyone and everything freeze — everything save his thoughts, and though he can write nothing down, he can mentally complete his play, and thus satisfy his personal goals despite the chaotic force ranged against him. Moreover, his play, entitled *The Enemies,* is full of incongruities, which in this case indicate that the drama has never taken place. Hladik wants to remind his audience that a play is unreal (thus he writes in verse), and that unreality is the necessary condition of art. It is also possible that Hladik's drama reassures him that the drama his real enemies have constructed for him has not taken place, and that Borges presents the impossible and untestable supposition that time freezes for a year to remind his audience that his own story is unreal.

Borges's most powerful, most human tale about the role of desire and hope in our confused and tenuous assessment of reality is 'The South'. In the prologue to the second part of *Fictions,* in which the tale appears, he suggests that this may be his best story, and it is certainly one which touches on important autobiographical details. Borges became delirious while suffering from septicaemia, and when he recovered he tested his intellectual abilities by constructing fictions, believing that the logic and rigour of fictions would be more demanding than any other mental exercise. 'The South' describes Dahlmann's sufferings during septicaemia and the fictions he constructs in convalescence, though Dahlmann's fictions are fantasies which prevent him from testing reality.

'The South' covers much the same human ground as does Heinrich Böll's non-fantastic tale 'Stranger Bear Word to the Spartans We ...' (1950) in *Children are Civilians Too* (1964). In Böll's story, a wounded soldier is carried along a corridor which has an unplaceable, dream-like familiarity. He thinks, but cannot quite believe, that it is his former school. The gentle rhythm of the stretcher, the fever and the pain, enclose him in memories which feel impossibly distant; yet, as he is placed on an operating table he sees the words of a Latin exercise still clearly written on the blackboard, as though his school days were still in process. This jarring sense of re-entering a past which has been cruelly disrupted is followed almost immediately by an image of a mangled, limbless body — an image which is the soldier's reflection in the operating mirror.

Böll does not use hallucination or dream, but the seductive musing, the confusion, and the realisation which breaks through without preparation, are similar to the pathetic gropings in fantasy literature in which the self is so often unknown and unacceptable. In 'The South' Borges also explores a feverish reaching-out towards life, which is far too tender to support the actuality that issues from the initial stirrings of consciousness. He describes the seductive fatigue of convalescence, the peculiar sensation of being protected, the intensified images and sluggish fascination with small things, the feebleness and apathy in drawing conclusions that accompany feverishness.

As with the soldier in Böll's tale, Dahlmann's realisation of his initial injury and the extent of his subsequent illness is brought about through reflections — in Dahlmann's case it is not a mirror that reflects his image, but other people's faces: 'In the obscurity, something brushed by his forehead: a bat, a bird? On the face of the woman who opened the door to him he saw horror engraved, and the hand he wiped across his face came away red with blood.'[25] The fear that something is happening to the self which is not understood increases the character's helplessness, and this confusion, this gap between awareness and injury dominates the tale.

In Dalhmann's eagerness to study the volume of *The Thousand and One Nights* he holds in his hand, he rushes up the stairs to his room. He bumps into a door, and from the wound develops septicaemia. When he recovers he decides to return to his ranch in the south. He is directed to get off the train at a station of which he has never heard, though he is assured that it is near his ranch. While he is seated at a table, reading *The Thousand and*

One Nights, a gaucho challenges him to fight, and the tale concludes as he walks out on the southern plain to defend himself with a knife he probably does not know how to wield.

It is never clear, however, whether Dahlmann actually does recover from his illness and journeys to the south, or whether the dream-like elements of the final episode with the gaucho — the unexpected descent at an unknown station, the local store-owner's unexplained knowledge of his name, the bread pellet thrown by the gaucho which hits him just where the door hit him — are part of a strange reality or part of a dream. In any case, Dahlmann accepts the events as his dream: if he had died of his illness, then this death, epitomising his South, is the death he would have dreamed.

The South is for Dahlmann a stern and ancient world. It offers him renewed vividness ('In the yellow light of the new day, all things returned to him.'[26]), yet this upsurge of life is also an upsurge of imagination and, like Sheherezade of whom he reads, Dahlmann is trapped between fantasy and death. Dahlmann's illness has broken down normal, human time. Sipping coffee in the station café, waiting for his train, he smoothes back the fur of a black cat and feels that the contact is illusory, for he is separated from it as though by glass; man lives in time, in succession, while the 'magical animal lives in the present, in the eternity of the instant'.[27] But Dahlmann cannot live in human successive time. Caught in his dreams, he lives simultaneous possibilities:

> *Tomorrow I'll wake up at the ranch,* he thought, and it was as if he was two men at a time: the man who travelled through the autumn day and across the geography of the fatherland, and the other one, locked up in a sanatorium and subject to methodical servitude. He saw unplastered brick houses, long and angled, timelessly watching the trains go by [. . .][28]

Dahlmann admires the stern and ancient qualities of his South, but when confronted with them, when forced to participate in them, he opts for the more meagre possibility: as he stoops to pick up the knife the gaucho throws to him, he thinks, *They would not have allowed such things to happen to me in the sanatorium.* But Dahlmann cannot escape. Imagination has claimed him and he must endure all its implications. His fantasy aims at perfect revelation, and the desires of the individual fantasiser are left behind.

The possibility that an encompassing and passably consistent dream — that is, a fantasy — can virtually replace reality, gives rise, by way of an idealist philosophy, to the possibility that the character himself is a product of another's imagination and, as such, has no existence independent of his creator's mind. In another story in *Fictions,* 'The Circular Ruins', Borges exploits this idea with magical effect. The protagonist's task is to search, by dreaming, for a worthy soul. After a false start, he tries again:

He understood that modelling the incoherent and vertiginous matter of which dreams are composed was the most difficult task that a man could undertake ... He swore he would forget the enormous hallucination which had thrown him off at first, and he sought another method of work. Before putting it into execution, he spent a month recovering his strength, which had been squandered by his delirium [...]

He dreamed that it was warm, secret, about the size of a clenched fist, and of a garnet colour within the penumbra of a human body as yet without face or sex; during fourteen lucid nights he dreamt of it with meticulous love. Every night he perceived it more clearly. He did not touch it; he only permitted himself to witness it, to observe it, and occasionally to rectify it with a glance. He perceived it and lived it from all angles and distances [...] He dreamed an entire man, a young man, but who did not sit up or talk, who was unable to open his eyes. Night after night, the man dreamt him asleep.

[...] Secretly, he was pained at the idea of being separated from him. On the pretext of pedogogical necessity, each day he increased the number of hours dedicated to dreaming. He also remade the right shoulder, which was somewhat defective. At times, he was disturbed by the impression that all this had already happened [...] In general, his days were happy; when he closed his eyes, he thought: *Now I will be with my son.* Or more rarely: *The son I have engendered is waiting for me and will not exist if I do not go to him.*[29]

The dreamer-creator wants to protect his 'son' from the knowledge that he is a phantom and fears fire, in particular, for the young man's immunity to fire will reveal the secret of his existence. It is, however, the dreamer himself who learns of his own unreality as his temple goes up in flames, which 'caressed him and flooded him without heat or combustion'. The dreamer is as much a phantom as his 'son': 'With relief, with humiliation, with terror, he understood that he also was an illusion, that someone else was dreaming him.'[30]

Borges returns to this theme in a later parable from *Dreamtigers*

(1964), 'Everything and Nothing', which describes a man's attempt (he is anonymous until the final sentence, in which his creator addresses him as 'Shakespeare') to escape his belief that he is no one, that he is merely 'a dream dreamt by no one'. He realises that not all men see themselves in this way and thus escapes his own unreality by assuming the identity of others. As an actor he has an identity and is temporarily satisfied, but, after twenty years of having been various kings and lovers, he returns home. As he dies he pleads with God: 'I who have been so many men in vain want to be one and myself,' but God answers him: 'Neither am I anyone; I have dreamt the world as you dreamt your work, my Shakespeare, and among the forms in my dream are you, who like myself are many and no one.'[31] Thus Borges links psychological and logical problems of self-identity. We see the former in Shakespeare's case, for it is tempting to suppose that a man whose imagination was so outrageously sympathetic, who understood all the implications of what it was to be so many different people, must identify himself with his characters; his imagination worked because he became them. God's problem, however, is a logical one: what test can a non-physical, unique, unknown being have of its own identity? Moreover, if He loves and understands His creations, as He is said to do, if He knows our every thought and wish directly, then how is He distinguishable from us, from the subjects of those thoughts and wishes. Borges's blasphemy is exceedingly subtle and exceedingly logical.

Yet Borges's theme of the dreamer as a phantom in another's dream, is not pursued as a testing ground for idealism. In Berkeley's world, for example, the dreamer in 'The Circular Ruins' would have been burnt by the flames, as would his 'son' if the dreamer himself had God's power. Idealism leaves natural laws where they stand, and one such law is that flesh will be burned by fire. The formulation of this natural law is based upon past experience, which is (and empiricists generally hold this belief) the only basis for our notions of cause and effect. What Borges does is to present a chink in the idealist world, one which would never be accepted by an idealist philosopher, and thus to show the strangeness of its suppositions. Moreover, if our identity, indeed our existence, depends upon God's perception-creation, then, as Borges indicates in 'Everything and Nothing', God's identity can be supposed to have a similar logic, and therefore He is only a dreamer, creating phantoms like himself.

The rigorous yet apparently ridiculous logic of Borges's work is distinctly reminiscent of Lewis Carroll. *Alice in Wonderland* tests and teases commonplace assumptions, and *Through the Looking-Glass* presents surprising and ingenious reversals (not merely negations) of ordinary expectations about the way the world works. In particular, Borges's use of the dream theme to confound a character with the possibility that he is an element in someone's dream, and as such is dependent for his very existence upon the dream, was employed by Lewis Carroll in Tweedledee's remark about the Red King's dream: the Red King is dreaming about Alice, and if he woke up, she would 'go out — bang! — just like a candle'. Nothing Alice says or does can contradict Tweedledee's claim, because everything she says or does is part of the Red King's dream. (Of course, the 'real' situation is that the Red King is an element in Alice's dream, and therefore Alice's dreaming about the possibility of the Red King dreaming her, is Lewis Carroll's presentation of the mirror image of Alice's dreaming of the Red King.)

Borges, however, is fascinated not only by logic, but also by the passion in fantasy, both as an activity and as a means of creating products to which his characters are emotionally attached. In one story, and one story only — 'Ulriche' from *The Book of Sand* — he presents fantasy as a direct means of fulfilling a sexual wish. The wry sadness of the ageing bachelor as, in embracing Ulriche he acknowledges that he embraces her image 'for the first and last time', indicates the role loneliness and desire have played in his fantasy, but the fascination of logic and psychology have proved to have no less force than these.

8 Psychoanalysis as Fantasy

Psychoanalysis, like fantasy literature, deals with those aspects of thought that tend to destroy, or at least to change, the rationalist's normality. Pathology does psychoanalysis the service of making discernible by isolation and exaggeration conditions which are ordinarily concealed or reduced. Fantasy can be seen as literature's counterpart to pathology; for though in literature fantasy has undergone conscious revision, it retains many characteristics (and, some analysts would maintain, the function) of primitive fantasy. Yet the aim of fantasy in the literature discussed here is, like the aim of psychoanalysis, the investigation of human reality. At the outset, then, is the paradox that terms which signal diversion from reality are the means by which reality is revealed.

Psychoanalysis began with the dispelling of this paradox. Freud discovered that his patients' apparently nonsensical behaviour had meaning and that, for various reasons, that meaning was hidden from the patients themselves. In uncovering the meaning of symptoms and the mechanisms by which their meaning was disguised, Freud postulated the wide-ranging influence of the unconscious in human behaviour and thus laid the groundwork for psychoanalytic theory. He discovered, too, that in speaking of their symptoms, patients tend to mention their dreams, and this led him to suspect that dreams had a meaning of similar kind.[1]

Fantasy's intimate link with the dream has already been mentioned. Often it shares the dream-like combination of vividness and vagueness, or the common dream impression of significance wedded either to nonsense or to the pedestrian. Also, it exhibits those characteristics Freud listed as the special features of the unconscious processes and which emerge in dreams: exemption from mutual contradiction, timelessness, replacement of external by internal reality, and a tendency for emotions suddenly to change both their character and their objects.[2] However, psychoanalytic methods of dream interpretation cannot, without due care and modification, be legitimately applied to fantasy literature, not only because the dreamer's free associations are either unavailable (if the dreamer is identified with the author) or non-existent (if the dreamer is identified with a character), but because careful readings of fantasy literature reveal the bias and limitations of psychoanalytic interpretations.

In *The Interpretation of Dreams* Freud insists that the ideas uncovered by free association, and by depth analysis in general, are 'undesired ideas' — undesired, that is, by the ego, but desired by the unconscious. The wish realised by the dream, however, is seldom straightforward. According to Freud, a conscious wish can become a dream-instigator only if it succeeds in awakening an unconscious wish which bears some similarity to and enforces the conscious wish. The dream itself can be considered a substitute for an infantile scene, modified by transference on to a recent experience. Thus the wish arising within the dream has been transferred to recent material; alternatively, a recent wish, having been suppressed, gains strength and reinforcement from the unconscious. The wish seeks the normal paths towards consciousness, but meets the censor, and at this point takes on the distortion which is already inherent in the transference of an infantile wish on to recent material. Owing to the peculiar nature of sleep, dream processes enter upon a regressive path, led along that path by memories, some of which exist only in visual form. Thus it is along its regressive path that the dream process acquires its representability.

The special characteristics of the dream also develop as a result of censorship; their purpose is to disguise the dream's meaning from the ego — i.e., from that part of the mind which confronts the external world and which is overseen by the super-ego. Symbolism (which is usually idiosyncratic, so that the meaning of an image cannot be discovered by reference to general meanings but to the free associations of the dreamer) aids this disguise, working alongside the censor to make the wish expressed within the dream unrecognisable. The analyst's task is to bring to light those thoughts and desires which are disguised by the dream work. Thus, unlike aesthetic imagery, dream imagery disguises rather than discloses its meaning. Moreover, Freud's description of symbolic relationships is adequate only for an exeedingly naïve allegory. Dream images, however diverse, have a narrow range of reference: they stand for the human body, as a whole or its parts, parents, children, brothers, sisters, birth, death, nakedness, sex organs and sexual activities. Images are chosen on the basis of some — or indeed any — similarity to the object or activity they represent. In themselves they are valueless, a key to be discarded when the analyst has opened the door.

Freud's actual analyses of dreams, however, are far more closely related to subtle readings of allegories and other genres than his theories themselves indicate. He rarely sticks by his crude pronouncements as to the scope of symbolic representation, nor are the details of his interpretations restricted by his theory that the dream is a hallucination of a wish as fulfilled. Many critics have already pointed out that terms describing the dream work (i.e., the processes by which the thoughts and wishes lying behind the dream are transformed into the dream the patient relates, or the manifest content of the dream) are analogous to literary techniques.[3] Displacement, or the shifting of emotional accent, condensation, or the conflation of several thoughts or characteristics, decomposition, or the breaking-up of a single thought or character, and over-determination, or the multiple causes and references of a single image, are familiar literary features. In fact, condensation and displacement are versions of metaphor and metonymy, the latter preceeding by (hidden) association of contiguous ideas, and the former uniting ideas on the basis of resemblance, whereas decomposition would result in synecdoche. (Indeed, the distinctly linguistic features of the mechanisms of the dream work, which is posited as residing in the unconscious, led Jacques Lacan to conclude that the unconscious is structured like a language.) Also, Freud's meticulous and creative attention to every detail must be admired by both the artist and critic.

Like an allegory the dream content is a series of hieroglyphs to be interpreted;[4] and, like any good allegory, the dream content cannot be read as a simple translation, nor can the various meanings be arranged like layers of a wedding cake, for the terms have cross-references and permit substitutions which themselves have cross-references. The differences between the dream and allegory show up not the dream's essential differences from literature but its peculiar kinship with fantasy. For, unlike an allegory, the dream content provides no rules for translation within the 'text', nor is there a generally consistent plane upon which the story, or stories, take place. The language of the dream is commonly pictorial, as it is in allegory, but sometimes the dream's primitive language is to be interpreted literarlly, sometimes figuratively, and the dream itself never indicates which interpretation is valid.[5] As in fantasy, we are neither in the world of concrete images nor of abstractions, but a middle ground in which literal language has an unreliable and unruly figurative tendency.

Generally in dreams we find ourselves in confusing situations. We no longer know our way about. The most commonplace occurrence may seem very odd or even terrifying. Whatever the visual similarity between the dream and the waking world, the images in the dream world are different. Verisimilitude is at best partially relevant, and usually fraudulent. Freud explained that dream images reveal the use of a primitive language, but in his analyses it is clear that however primitive the terms of the language, the associations may be primitive and infantile, mature, or quite ordinary. In the dream of Irma's injection, for example, the people represent themselves, while their diseases and attitudes challenge Freud's responsibility and reputation precisely as they do in waking life, on rational grounds. If Freud has mis-diagnosed Irma's condition as hysterical, allowing an organic condition to worsen, then he holds himself responsible, as will others. On the other hand, if Irma's complaint is organic, Freud's psychoanalytic techniques are not put into question by their failure to cure her. The slippery logic of the apparently absurd conversation in this dream is similar to the apparent *non sequiturs* in George Bandemann's conversation with his father, when hidden emotions guide every topic of discussion. In Freud's dream Dr M. says, 'There's no doubt that it's an infection, but it doesn't matter; dysentery will follow and the poison will be eliminated.' The remark, 'It doesn't matter', is spotted by Freud as a suspect consolation. He begins to see, as he dreams, that the supposition of the patient's organic sufferings is an attempt to shift blame from himself for not being able to cure her. His dream-self knows that he has imagined her organic sufferings; to imagine something, in the dream world, is to put it into effect, and, therefore, the sleeping Freud believes he has given Irma her organic symptoms. Thus he needs to be reassured that the outcome of the illness is benign. In sleep Freud makes the mistake Schwartz's Frank Lawrence makes, with less impact and plausibility, in waking: he is responsible for dream occurrences in the way he would be for instigating actual conditions.

Dr M.'s remarks console Freud for his supposition (infliction) of Irma's sufferings; but, simultaneously, they cast aspersion on Dr M., for the prognosis he offers as consolation is nonsensical. Freud both uses and rejects his colleague's comments in much the same way Kafka's George Bandemann simultaneously mocks and embraces his father. The dream of Irma's injection is highly 'realistic'. Freud's narrative does not depend upon the primitive language of images, nor his interpretation upon primitive meanings. The dream deals with problematic and indeed quite sophisticated issues of guilt and egoism in conditions, so familiar to the fantasist, of being unable to mark boundaries between autonomous and intentional occurrences. It begins to map out unexpected areas of responsibility and paths of evasion. This dream can be seen as an incipient fantasy tale.

Naturally many of the dreams Freud discusses are more primitive than 'Irma's injection', but they all depend upon a well-developed appreciation of language and its aesthetic function. 'Letting off steam' may be represented by a radiator, thus employing in pictorial imagery the common and less-comic figure of speech; the image depends upon ordinary language, even as it defies ordinary rules of language. Freud's view of aesthetic uses of language was essentially Aristotle's, who considered them to be 'pleasurable accessories' to the business of verbal representation. Freud believed that pleasures were ploys to distract attention from the true aim of representation — viz., the enactment of forbidden, or repressed, desires; aesthetic pleasures disguised the real objects of pleasure and made it possible for them to be enjoyed. Freud failed to see that those qualities which made certain kinds of representation possible were, by virtue of that capacity, aesthetic qualities. He assumed that in so far as images were functional they were non-aesthetic, whereas the reverse is true: aesthetic is function. Thus, in describing the complex associations of images and patterns, he was pointing precisely to their aesthetic features. Similarly, he often ignored the aesthetic impact of the dreams he related. Even the simple dream of convenience in which, being thirsty, he dreams that his wife is offering him a drink from an Etruscan cinerary urn (which he had recently given away), displays an eloquence and economy of meaning. Regret for the loss of the vase and the need for water are presented in the dream as fulfilled desires (he has the vase and is drinking), but these are only part of the 'story'. The graciousness of his wife's administration, complemented by the lovely vase, expresses tenderness and calm alongside the regret, which mitigates Freud's egostic interpretation. It expresses, moreover, something of the quality of Freud's feelings for his wife: such a dream, as related, would not be had by a man who disrespected, distrusted or resented his wife's attentions. And all of this is absent from Freud's analysis; he stops when he has the patterns and associations necessary to support his theory, thus begging the question of its centrality.

In many of his dream analyses, however, Freud does pay attention to those features which could be classified as aesthetic, if only to explain why it is they do not arouse, within the dream, the expected associations. As he discusses the dream in which he urinates over a bench covered in excrement, washing it clean with the stream of urine, satisfied with his task but also having the impression that something remained, he questions why it is he experienced no disgust in the dream. He concludes that the dream represented himself as Hercules cleansing the stables (of ignorance and prejudice), thus providing an analogue to his own work on the infant aetiology of neurosis (and thus preventing his own children from falling ill). Yet even as Freud explains the absence of aesthetic purport of these images — i.e., their inherently disgusting features — he does not neglect them. The purpose of the images was to express both self-glorification (himself as Hercules) and self-depreciation (he had been bothered, the previous day, by a sycophantic member of his lecture audience). Thus the excrement and urine do retain their usual associations; their function here is to denigrate Freud's task, even as he glorifies it. More importantly and disturbingly, it may indicate what Freud thought he was doing in analysis: did he consider the repressed desires and beliefs he dealt with to be excrement, and was his analysis, or the motive of his analysis, roughly of the same quality?

Freud himself, in discussing the dream of Irma's injection, maintained that the task of drawing associations in the unconscious could be endless. Thus the range of possible interpretations is vast, and suggestions for alternative interpretations do not necessarily contradict his own. However, given the flexibility and open-endedness of interpretation, it would seem that any general theory as to the purpose and nature of dreams could be supported by dream interpretation. The very brilliance and breadth of Freud's interpretations challenge the authority of his theory. Moreover, they challenge the adequacy of the referents he lists for dream symbols; for, given the ramification and proliferation of associations, it would seem that the human body, parents, children, brothers, sisters, nakedness, sex organs and sexual activity also have allusive power. As Lacan notes in *Ecrits,* even the phallus, so often designated as the referent of a dream image, is not the organ itself but the *simulacrum* of the ancients and itself a signifier. What Freud convinces us of in *The Interpretation of Dreams* is that dream images have meaning, and that their meaning emerges in a variety of ways, and, moreover, that their meaning is the motive of their formation. He also succeeds in convincing us that his theory can be applied to any dream, but not that the application reveals the dream's central meaning.

Freud showed that the strange representation of familiar objects is a common enterprise; we all experience it and participate in it by dreaming. He showed, too, that the motive for these strange representations was linked to their meaning, that dream fantasies revealed and sought out meanings. Normally, in waking life, we can discard this strangeness. Fantasy literature re-asserts its importance and shows it, as does Freud, to be a means of focusing the difficulties in perception, knowledge and emotion which often cannot be differentiated by ordinary language. Thus the fantasist must part company with Freud in his supposition that imagery is a disguise and that absurdity and anxiety, too, are effects of censorship. For anxiety in fantasy literature, and quite possibly in the dream, is often part and parcel of the strangeness represented therein. The absurdity we discover to be a valid means of representing our world defies common presuppositions. The knowledge of generalities which makes us confident adults either functions haphazardly or piecemeal. In such transformed circumstances anticipation is bound to be both inaccurate and ineffective. Anxiety arises from the new, confusing perspectives. Thus Freud misses this realistic impact of dream characteristics when he interprets absurdity and anxiety in accord with his theory of the dream as a hallucinated fulfilment of a wish motivated by the desire to maintain sleep, wherein absurdity is a means of rejecting the content of the dream (thus endorsing the wish that one is not enjoying what one is in fact enjoying), and anxiety indicates either an unsuccessful disguise of the wish from the ego or the ego's own wish to be punished.

Fantasy investigates, among other things, fears and wishes and the strange relation between the two, a relation coloured by ambivalence, self-ignorance and simplicity. There is no point in granting dominance to the wish. William Golding's *Pincher Martin* is a fantasy novel that might, according to psychoanalytic theory, be construed as a hallucination based upon a wish: a drowning man imagines that he is on a deserted island and that he is fighting against great odds to survive. The wish underlying the fantasy is that he has a chance to survive, that intelligence and determination may be of use to him; whereas he is in fact drowning. Pincher Martin's fantasy is not that of surviving in easy circumstances, which it might as well be, if wish-fulfilment is the point of fantasy. Yet psychoanalytic interpretations have never supposed that wishes are realised without impediments. Dreams, like neurotic symptoms, are the products of conflict and compromise between the primary unconscious impulses and the secondary conscious ones. Often the dreams Freud relates acknowledge a good deal of harsh reality, seeming, in fact, to ask, 'Given that this is what is known and confronted, how can the fulfilment of a desire be imagined?' In the final chapter of *The Interpretation of Dreams* Freud reports a hauntingly sad dream of a father whose child had died. Having watched day and night beside the child's sick bed, the man was tired, and so lay down in a room adjoining that in which the child lay, leaving the door ajar so that he could see the tall candles surrounding the body. An old man remained beside the dead child as watcher, murmuring prayers. After sleeping a few hours the father dreamed that his child was standing beside his bed, clasping his hands and crying reproachfully, 'Father, don't you see that I am burning?' The father woke and noticed that the watcher had fallen asleep, and that a candle had fallen on to his dead child, burning one arm.

The wish fulfilled here, Freud argues, is that the child appears alive, and it is for the sake of the living vision that the father sleeps a moment longer rather than waking to attend to the fire. Yet the father's dream, like Pincher Martin's hallucination, investigates, whatever else is also does, the appalling reality. That image of the reproachful, burning child (worthy of Emily Brontë) alludes to the outraged and useless paternal protectiveness, to his continuing tenderness for the dead body, to his uncertainty as to the meaning of death. Though Freud himself would not necessarily deny the validity of these allusions (he maintains that the task of discovering associations may be endless), his theory denies their centrality. However, even in the fragmented and unrevised dream, fantasy reveals an impulse and capacity for exploring unpleasant realities. Accordingly, Pincher Martin's hallucination need not be construed as a wish disguised as an investigation of realistic potential. It can be viewed as a comment upon the impetus of fantasy, which presents various phenomena, both possible and impossible, in order to consider further possibilities or to explore implications of reality. Naturally this can be done well, or it can be done badly. Freud's ingenuity was such that he was able to detect the pattern of poor fantasy even in good fantasy.

Psychoanalytic theory does not deny, but stresses the role fantasy plays in the apprehension of reality. Thus Lionel Trilling, while declaring that Freud does not have the proper 'feel' of literature, points out that he nonetheless has a special affiliation with literature, and indeed with art in general, because he views the mind as a fantasy-producing mechanism.[6] In 'Formulations on the Two Principles of Mental Functioning' (1911), and in his papers on narcissism and negation, Freud, with the careless grandeur of the speculator, presents his theory of the primacy of fantasy. The sovereign tendency of the primary mental processes, which form the larger part of the unconscious, is the pleasure principle; that is, these processes either strive, independently and immediately, towards the satisfaction of some need, or flee from some pain. Initially fantasy — in the form of hallucinatory wish-fulfilment — is the sole form of mental activity. The aim of the first psychic activity is to produce a repetition of the perception which was linked with the satisfaction of a need; the psychical activity was to produce a 'perceptual identity' between the hallucination and that which previously brought satisfaction.[7] Thus hallucination turns away from reality and generates a metaphor: the thought is like the external object which satisfied the need. This, the shortest path to satisfaction, is discovered to be a false path. In circumventing reality, in attempting to make the external internal by hallucination, desires are frustrated rather than satisfied. We turn from fantasy towards reality not in conflict but in accord with the pleasure principle; we learn that to satisfy desires we must plan and act, deferring immediate gratification. Nonetheless, a residue of hallucinatory activity is split off, kept free from reality-testing, remaining subordinate to the pleasure principle alone. This residual activity, which functions as a compensation for the normal dominance of the reality principle, is fantasy; and it is the artist's special function to indulge this compensatory activity.

Psychoanalytic theory aims to investigate a wide range of mental phenomena, and the controlled imaginative product is not its main subject; but art's special relevance to the relation between fantasy and reality links it with the central issues of psychoanalysis, and makes Freud's assessment of the artist's motives and the function of his products particularly provoking. His best-known pronouncement on these matters is that

> An artist is originally a man who turns away from reality because he cannot come to terms with the renunciation of instinctual satisfaction which it at first demands, and who allows his erotic and ambitious wishes full play in the life of phantasy by making use of special gifts to mould his phantasies into truths of a new kind which are valued by men as precious reflections of reality. Thus in a certain fashion he actually becomes the hero, the king, the creator, or the favourite he desired to be, without following the long roundabout path of making real alterations in the external world. But he can only achieve this because other men feel the same dissatisfaction as he does with the renunciation demanded by reality, and because that dissatisfaction, which results from the replacements of the pleasure principle by the reality principle, is itself a part of reality.[8]

Clearly Freud does not identify the artist with the neurotic who abandons the reality principle, but he does identify the artist's work with imagined gratification, a pretence of actual satisfaction, as in primitive fantasy. Though he acknowledges that many writers are far removed from the model of the naïve day-dream, he suspects that even the most extreme deviations from the model could be linked to it through an uninterrupted series of transitional cases.[9] Fantasy in art remains independent of reality; it is the fact of fantasy in mental life which persuades people to view them as reflections upon actual life.

Since the art work permits satisfaction of unconscious and repressed desires, it must diguise the gratification it provides so that resistances are kept at bay and forbidden satisfactions are enjoyed without arousing the anxiety that it is repression's purpose to prevent. In 'Psychopathic Characters on the Stage' (1915) Freud suggests that the function of aesthetic features is to disguise and distract the audience from its real objects of enjoyment. This paper complements his earlier 'Creative Writers and Day-Dreaming' (1908) in which the poet's special, inexplicable skill was to present his own erotic and ambitious wishes in a way that made them attractive to others, who are usually repelled by someone else's egoistic fantasies. Here the supposition is that the audience is persuaded to accept the author's imagined wish-fulfilment as their own. In 'Psychopathic Characters' the enjoyment is seen to arise from the audience's participation in the characters' neuroses. Even though the characters themselves may be unhappy, they have the freedom to enact or at least to brood upon desires which the (hypothetically normal) audience suppresses. Thus the audience, secretly sharing the characters' complexes, enjoys the play.

A few years later, however, in *Beyond the Pleasure Principle*, Freud drew a connection between art and children's play whose aim, in its repetitiveness, is to master a previous experience before which one was passive. The repetition compulsion, he believed, also explained the pleasure we take in the painful emotions expressed in art: the audience is relieved, by the enactment of their unconscious desires, of the need for repression, which signals passivity in regard to those emotions. Thus for the first time Freud proposed fantasy as a means of mastering, rather than evading, problematic emotions. Unfortunately, in his theory the notion of mastery remains a function of mere repetition or, at best, as the acquisition of a skill. The crucial methods of mastering — elaboration and investigation — which indicate fantasy's aims, are ignored.

Followers of Freud have employed their own definitions of symbolism to explain the development of primary fantasying into reality-testing. Ernest Jones[10] shares Freud's assumption that symbolism is the substitution of one term for another and that the similarity between two ideas allows one to function as though it were identical to the other. The tendency (of the primitive, not the adult or conscious mind) to identify one thing with another stems from mental sluggishness. To make a new object or idea easier to comprehend, it is equated with something already known. Thus, while widening knowledge, we remain in a familiar sphere.

Jones narrows Freud's general account of the basis upon which one idea becomes a symbol for another, whereby shape, material, function, contiguity in space or time may equally indicate the decisive, symbol-forming similarity. Jones believes that one object or idea is identified with another not on the basis of objective qualities but on the basis of our interest in it. Since the interest will be primarily libidinous, and since the libidinous interests are repressed, the symbol signals repression: only those similes in which one term is unconscious become symbols; and symbolism, in harmony with the pleasure principle (emerging here both as mental inertia in the face of new ideas and as the basis upon which ideas are related), provides the means of making new realities acceptable. We do not have to work too hard to understand them, and they appear pleasurable in the light of the pleasures with which we associate them.

Melanie Klein also views fantasy as the instigator of reality-investigation.[11] Accepting Ferenczi's theory that identification, the forerunner of symbolism, arises from the infant's attempt to rediscover in every object his or his parents' organs and their functions, and accepting Jones's view that objects or ideas are equated on the basis of similar pleasures offered, Klein postulates symbolism, and the fantasies surrounding symbolism, as the foundation of all interest and activity. Alongside the libidinal interest we take in objects (identifying them with organs and their functions), is the anxiety which arises in the oral-sadistic phase. Since during that phase the infant wants to destroy the organs (penis, vagina, breast — all, in the infant's view, belonging to the mother) with which external objects are identified, he fears retaliation for these desires and develops a dread of the objects thus associated. To avoid anxiety, he turns to new objects, but any object interests him only because it is identified with organs and their functions. Thus, the new objects soon (but, in normal children, not too soon) also arouse anxiety, and once again new objects must be sought and new associations learned as a protection against anxiety.

Fantasy, therefore, in Klein's view, is crucial to the apprehension of reality, yet reality-interest arises as a defence against our primary interests. It is not by means of fantasy that reality is discovered but as a by-product of and defence against fantasy. Thus, though these psychoanalytic theories grant primacy to fantasy in mental life, they do not — with the important exception of Freud's postulation of the repetition compulsion — suggest how fantasy itself can test reality.

Recently D.W. Winnicott has offered a more sympathetic account of fantasy's role in the acceptance, if not the testing, of reality.[12] He suggests that the gap between the objective and external on the one hand, and subjectivity and imagination on the other, is both bridged and formed (the distinction between reality and imagination is formed at the same time it is accepted) by transitional phenomena, so called because they represent the infant's transition from being merged with the mother to relating to her as a separate and external person. The transitional object (the blanket, toy or whatever) represents a part-object, such as the breast; but what is as important as its symbolic value is its actuality: the object is real, not hallucinated, and when the child creates a symbol from the object, he already knows the difference between reality and illusion. The transitional object makes the distinction acceptable, because it allows the outer world to bear the characteristics of the inner one.

Winnicott explicitly denigrates fantasy, distinguishing it from dream which issues in play and therefore in action: fantasy is negative, impeding action and evading life. His distinction, however, is a technical, not conceptual definition. He slights only that fantasy which does not lead to activity, and calls 'fantasy' only those imaginings which are unrelated to life. Moreover, his conflation of the objective and external, his supposition that these are firmly distinct from the subjective, with the related assumption that the attribution of affect to external objects is projection, are too simplistic to make his model useful. 'Inner' and 'outer' are not always distinguishable: we see the sadness in, not behind the face, and an ability to see external beings as feeling beings involves objective knowledge. Since he supposes that the internal and external are bridged by projection, and ignores the way in which the character of the external or 'objective' can specifically indicate subjective facts, Winnicott, like Jones and Klein, sees fantasy's aims as adaptive, with investigation as merely its by-product. Fantasy — or in Winnicott's terminology, the dream — may lead to play, to experimentation and investigation, but in his model its suppositions may be peeled off from reality, leaving it untouched. Nothing about the blanket or toy, after all, is revealed by an investigation of the child's fantasy.

The most influential and popular psychoanalytic proponent of fantasy's usefulness is undoubtedly Carl Jung. Many artists, including Nabokov and Borges, find Jung's theories of imagination's function and purpose more relevant than those of the Freudian school. Indeed, Jung does appear to grant fantasy, and the imagination in general, intelligent aims and apprehensions. Distinguishing between the personal and collective unconscious, he allows for a difference to be drawn between those images which arise from specific, personal desires and those which have more general meaning — not because they satisfy the audience's personal desires as well as the author's, but because they express or depict a range of interests and needs which may well not be related to desire but to a more complex concept of good.

Jung is aware, as many other psychoanalytic critics are not, that his literary interpretations set one story alongside another and aim at choosing an appropriate, enlightening metaphor rather than an explanation in terms of personal history. The referents of images and patterns, in cases where they arise from the collective unconscious, are primordial and archetypal. They are always unconscious, and therefore beyond description. Every interpretation, he declares, remains in the form 'as if': interpretations are always analogous.[13] Jung's recognition, however, leads to complacency about the accuracy of proffered interpretations. Vagueness is central to his tenets, as is indiscipline, since even the given work is only an approximation to unconscious meaning, and any other story, bearing any similarity to it, may be cited as relevant. It is as though Freud's highly general account of symbolism were made applicable to critical interpretation without the discipline of free association. Thus Jung's generalities destroy the work as much as to do Freud's specifications. Jung's endorsements of the mysterious and fantastic are fundamentally platitudinous, neglecting as they do the artist's specific aims and rigorously drawn distinctions.

Jung's theories are best applied to the visionary rather than to the fantasist. He believes that the mind, with the particular help of the imagination, is essentially self-regulating. Bias, exaggeration, distortion are viewed as unconscious regulating functions. Jung's model of the imagination is of a mechanism stimulated by the need to balance, warn or correct. Imagination does not aim towards the revelation of truths of this world but towards universal truths, which are really hopeful and harmonious visions taking their particular forms from the deficiencies of this world. Jung's optimism is thus at odds with the pathetic and defeatist struggle of the fantasist, for whom confusion, deception and imbalance are the targets of investigation.

The fantasist's world is also Freud's world; and Freud, the greatest representative of psychoanalysis, is also among the greatest fantasists. Within the scope of his powerful vision the obvious and normal lose their secure outlines. The patterns of association and development he describes proceed according to new rules whose ramifications must be painstakingly and ingeniously discovered. Thus he exhibits the fantasist's special task of teasing out possibilities beyond the point of absurdity alongside the compulsion to makes sense of the absurdity. Like Borges, Freud draws unexpected, unbelievable and irrefutable designs which can be skilfully superimposed upon the world we thought we knew. Once seen, these new patterns and associations can never be forgotten. Like all great writers, Freud creates his own predecessors, and a multitude of writers seem to bear his mark.

Freud believed that mental phenomena behave according to rules and that psychoanalysis could discover those rules. However, this aim is impeded by the mind's self-disguise. The analyst confronts deceptive and disconcerting material, full of mistaken leads and misguided expectations. The fantastic terrain of his territory is reflected in his language. In discussing the effects of repression in the psychoneuroses he writes:

> It shows us, for instance, that the instinctual presentation develops with less interference and more profusely if it is withdrawn by repression from conscious influence. It proliferates in the dark, as it were, and takes on extreme forms of expression, which, when translated and presented to the neurotic are not only bound to seem alien to him, but terrify him by giving him the picture of an extra-ordinary and dangerous strength of instinct. This deceptive strength of instinct is the result of an uninhibited development in phantasy of the damming-up consequent on frustrated satisfaction.[14]

Thus the patient, seeking help from the analyst, further confounds his task. Indeed, in *The Interpretation of Dreams,* Freud concluded that patients were reporting dreams which appeared to defy his theory of the dream as a hallucination of a wish as fulfilled, in order to challenge his theory: such dreams did present a wish, viz., the wish that Freud's theory was false. Freud's loyalty to his theories is sometimes comic, but it arises from the nature of his enterprise, which is to discover the rules of mind with tools that belong to mind, itself bent upon disguising those rules and able to enlist on its behalf the very tools which set out to investigate it.

In analysing fantasies Freud must construct fantasies. Only such constructions can frighten the necessary material from its various hiding places. The hypothesis of primary fantasy itself employs fantasy. The discussion of primary processes attempts to posit a mental state before there were any of those compromise structures of the psyche which arise from the transformation of one order of representation into another. But Freud must use images to explain the pre-compromise structure, images which are themselves compromise structures. Not only the language and theories Freud employs, but also the content of his interpretations employ fantasy, for only by appealing to fantasies can responses be explained. For example, children respond to their parents as though they were royalty or monsters; and these responses, based upon fantasies, are indicated in the special but realistic attachments and tensions between children and parents. To hypothesise, as Melanie Klein does, an objective capacity for challenging and taming these subjective beliefs (or imagoes) is not only to override Freud's theory that objectivity itself is based upon fantasy (the acceptance of a proposition, or the belief in its truth, is derived from the tendency to incorporate within the self or to devour, whereas the rejection of a proposition, or the belief that it is false, is derived from the tendency to expel from the body) but also to neglect the fact that a fully objective view of one's parents would be abnormal.

Among the mass of Freud's work which exhibits the priority of fantasy in psychological reality and, simultaneously, the use of fantasy in psychoanalytic hypotheses, is the case history known as the 'Wolf-Man.'[15] This, one of Freud's most famous cases, was published in 1918, when he was fighting the 'heresies' of Jung and Adler; the former saw phylogenetic factors as the most powerful determinants of human behaviour, and the latter cited the ego's struggle for power as the single drive or instinct. Thus both challenged Freud's insistence that the infantile factor plays a decisive part in determining whether and at what point the individual shall fail to master the real problems of life. Freud acknowledges the influences of both phylogenetic factors and egoism in this case-history but refers to the former only when every other possibility has been investigated, and sees the later as merely a stage in a more complete analysis.

'From the History of an Infantile Neurosis' thus treats every point with particular care. It can be seen as an approach to the question: what reality lies behind the patient's fantasy? Freud's reply suggests that the psychoanalyst's fantasy is the bedrock of psychological reality. This case-history reads as a delightful example of the fantasy-detective-tale. The only element out of place is Freud's thoroughly non-ironic attitude towards his analysis; for though some of his explanations are somewhat apologetic, his apologies are actually refusals to give way. Considering the possibility that the primal scene — which he describes in detail, specifying its time and place, and which, he maintains, underlies the patient's childhood nightmare — is either the patient's fantasy or his own (for he admits that many primal scenes, i.e., the earliest experiences of childhood brought to light in analysis, are not actual occurrences but products of the imagination which serve as representations of real wishes and interests), he reminds the reader of his meticulous piecing-together of the material and of the unpleasantness of the conclusions, which show that he was forced to his conclusions — as though a well-constructed fiction, fashioned by intelligent imagination and experience rather than by a fastidious taste and conscious decision, were not a fiction! At the same time, he recognises that a judgement against its reality would not disturb his analysis and subsequently justifies the fantastical quality of his work: 'The description of such early phases and of such deep strata of mental life has been a task which has never before been attacked; and it is better to perform that task badly than to take flight before it . . .'[16] He understands that he must proceed by means of fantastic constructions, yet repeats his low opinion of the aims of fantasies: they efface the memory of an event or disguise its significance or deny desires; they seek, also, to hide their very existence — as, in this case-history, do the boy's dreams of aggression against his sister, which screen his memory of being seduced (and humiliated) by her; the fantasy of his aggressiveness hides his own passivity.

The case history of the 'Wolf-Man' is that of an anxiety-hysteria in the form of animal phobia suffered by a boy from his fourth birthday to the age of about eight. His case was analysed initially by Freud fifteen years after its termination. A number of symptoms, some of which appeared to be contradictory, were explained, along with their (hypothetical) inter-relations. The boy's mother was, throughout his childhood, ill and he was therefore cared for by a nurse and, subsequently, also by an English governess. He was such a compliant and gentle child that he was frequently told that he should have been the girl, and his lively older sister should have been the boy. He was also told that he was his father's child — that is, his father's favourite — and this pleased him, for though towards the end of childhood he became estranged from his (manic-depressive) father, Freud's analysis shows that he wanted to be born of his father. The boy's illness, or its symptoms, began when his parents arrived home from their usual summer holiday. He became unmanageable, discontented and violent. According to the patient's memory, however, his disturbed behaviour first occurred on Christmas Day. He was upset that he had not received a double quantity of presents, which was his due, since Christmas Eve was also his birthday. Yet he could not arrange other pathological phenomena in temporal sequence. He recollected an awful fear of a wolf in a picture book, represented as standing upright and striding along; he would scream that the wolf was coming to eat him. He was frightened of all animals, regardless of their size, yet he also enjoyed harming them. This phase was replaced, under the influence of his mother, by pronounced piety. Instead of refusing to go to sleep for fear he would dream of wolves, he performed pious rites before bedtime. His pious phase, however, was accompanied by compulsive blasphemy. For example, he would feel obliged to think of the Holy Trinity every time he saw three heaps of excrement lying on the road.

Initially suspicion as to the cause of his illness fell upon the governess, because his behaviour deteriorated soon after her arrival and because she created tension in the house, with her antagonism towards the boy's well-loved nurse. In analytic sessions he recalled the governess walking in front of him and saying, 'Do look at my little tail!' Also, he remembered her hat flying off in the wind, to his great satisfaction. Freud suggested to him that these were screen memories for a castration fear, that the governess had threatened him in a way to arouse fear of castration, which might account for his abnormal behaviour. The analyst's suggestion brought forth memories of dreams of aggression against his sister, and Freud then concluded that these dreams indicated fantasies of the boy's aggressiveness, fantasies which disguised memories of his sister's humiliating seductions. Freud believed that the fantasy in this strand of the patient's history stopped here: the sister's seduction is supposed actually to have taken place.

The boy rejected his sister's advances partly because she was a rival to his parents' love, but he did not reject the (passive) pleasure she offered him. He sought another sexual object — his nurse — and, in an attempt to seduce her, began playing with his penis in her presence. The nurse told him he was naughty, and that he should be aware of being wounded as a result of onanism. Thus it was his nurse, not the governess, who threatened him. The governess's hostility towards the nurse made him exaggerate his love for the other woman, though, because of the nurse's rejection (scolding, threat), he was forced to seek a new sexual object. Since his first experience — and the experience he sought to repeat — was passive (viz., his sister touching his genitals), he sought a male object — his father, though this new object was, in fact, a return to the initial, dominating love object. After the nurse's threat, he gave up onanism; and his sexual life, which was just coming into the genital phase, was thrown back to the earlier phase of pre-genital organisation. The child's sexual life took on a sadistic-anal character. His sadism, which was expressed in his pleasure in tormenting animals, was in part revenge upon the nurse but it was also an attempt to kill all babies (represented by small animals), who would not only be rivals to his father's love but would also be a gift to him, a gift the son could not provide; or the babies could be viewed as a gift from the father, which the son could not receive. The anal language in which his sadism found expression also emerged in his attitude towards money, for since babies are gifts and money is associated with gifts, they are all identified, in Freud's theories, with faeces, which are seen as the child's first gift, a relinquishing of part of his body as a love-offering. (Moreover, because the column of faeces is felt as part of the infant's body, it becomes a prototype of the penis. The patient's blasphemous identification of God and faeces was as affectionate as it was abusive.)

Thus was the patient thrown into a jealous rage when he saw his father give his sister two bank notes: he felt his father had given her the babies he desired. When his sister died he rejoiced in the fact that her wealth was now his: for now his father would give babies to him alone and would, accordingly, offer him the anal sexual satisfaction he craved. The analysis is based upon Freud's theories of infants' beliefs about anatomy and conception, beliefs which allegedly abide in the unconscious.

The sadism that was directed against small creatures was also directed against the patient himself, taking a masochistic form. He enjoyed fantasies of being beaten, and when his father returned from his summer holiday he behaved badly in order to be beaten by him as a passive form of sexual satisfaction. Beating would, moreover, alleviate his guilt for his desires.

Freud's narration cannot be disengaged from his psychoanalytic interpretation. The placing of the dream in the child's history is also a citing of causes as opposed to effects, as of course is the placing of the primal scene. Thus do explanations create and mould the material they explain. Probabilities and plausibilities gauged from Freud's clinical experience and analytic theories play a large part in his reconstructions, which fill in gaps or extend the material provided by the patient: the story itself is fashioned by psychoanalytic theory. Freud is meticulous in his treatment of detail, yet many of the details are themselves fantastical constructions, and many omissions supplied by Freud are also created by him, owing to the type of pattern he considers complete. Many different patterns could be revealed, and a number of interpretations would be in accord with psychoanalytic theory.[17] Moreover, a number of commonsense elements are omitted, such as the child's possible anger at his parents for abandoning him on their holiday, and the role his mother's illness (and subsequent neglect) might have played in his object choice. (Indeed, Freud does not mention, as the Wolf-Man maintains in his memoirs, that his parents' return had been postponed.) The psychoanalytic theory of multi-determinacy should not be used to accept any alternative interpretation. Multiple associations or allusions cannot abolish logic, and contradictory explanations are acceptable only if the contradiction can either be dispelled or viewed as an expression of ambivalence. If the theory is not handled carefully, it obliterates the initially rigorous aims of psychoanalysis, making way for vague and complacent inconsequence.

Freud's analysis is only one possible interpretation, not because many others might be true according to the theory of over-determination of symptoms, but because of the sort of thing analysis is: it enlightens one story by means of another story, and the range of possibly enlightening stories is vast. (Psychoanalysis can also offer unenlightening stories, though Freud himself usually does not.) Thus, as a fantasist with a penchant for the Gothic, he pursues those elements which strike his interest. The following dream related by the patient, becomes central to his interpretation:

> I dreamt that it was night and that I was lying in my bed. (My bed stood with its foot towards the window; in front of the window there was a row of old walnut trees. I know it was winter when I had the dream, and night-time.) Suddenly the window opened of its own accord, and I was terrified to see that some white wolves were sitting on the big walnut tree in front of the window. There were six or seven of them. The wolves were quite white, and looked more like foxes or sheepdogs, for they had big tails like foxes and they had their ears pricked like dogs when they pay attention to something. In great terror, evidently of being eaten up by the wolves, I screamed and woke up.[18]

Since the wolves are watching something, it can be assumed that the infantile memory to which the dream is linked involves the dreamer watching something. (The unconscious language contains no negative terms and thus commonly presents a phenomenon as its opposite.) Since the wolves are motionless, it can be assumed that the object of the dreamer's attention consisted of violent motion. The material brought forward from the patient's and analyst's memories of fairy tales, shows that the wolf is castrated or castrating and voracious. The manifest dream tries to render the dream thoughts harmless; the fox-tails on the wolves are compensations for taillessness (i.e., castration), a representation derived from the grandfather's story of the tailor who pulled off the wolf's tail. The numbers six and seven are derived from 'The Seven Little Goats', in which six and seven appear, since there were seven goats but only six were eaten by the wolf. The parents are represented by the wolves in connection with their positions in the primal scene. Voraciousness is attributed to the father because he tended to engage in affectionate abuse, threatening, in fun, to 'gobble up' his son — or so Freud concludes from his interpretation of the patient's tranference. The fear of being eaten by the wolf is translated into a fear of copulation with the father. The desire becomes a fear, because the child, identifying himself with his mother (because she possesses the father), sees the castration he attributes to her as a prerequisite of his satisfaction.

The wishes which act as motive forces in this dream are, first, that

Christmas, with its presents, is here, and, secondly, that the dreamer is sexually satisfied by the father, a wish replaced by the desire to see once again the fascinating scene which showed what satisfaction from his father was like. This last wish, however, gives way to its repudiation and repression, the driving force of which is a narcissistic genital libido. The concern for his male organ was fighting against a satisfaction whose attainment seemed to involve the renunciation of that organ, for the woman who could receive the man was presumed to be castrated. Thus the child fled from his father to the less-dangerous nurse. Yet the desire remained sufficiently strong to revive the long-forgotten scene in which he discovered what sexual satisfaction from his father was like. This scene, Freud believes, is reproduced in the dream.

The reconstructed scene is this: when the patient was about eighteen months old he slept, owing to his illness, in his parents' room; one summer day he witnessed, at about five o'clock in the afternoon (the time of day his depression was particularly severe), his parents' *coitus a tergo,* repeated three times. The position of his father was recalled in his response to the upright wolf in the picture book. The wolves are white because the parents were in their underclothes; and the fact that they were thus attired, along with information about the child's health, leads Freud to place the scene in midsummer rather than in winter, when the dream takes place. The setting of the dream relates it to Christmas only in regard to the patient's disappointed expectation — he did not receive a double quantity of presents, a regret which is a screen for his frustrated anal desires. His parents' intercourse is translated into the wolves of his dream; and as he had identified with the castrated and passive mother, he wakes in terror of being 'eaten' — that is, castrated. For even at eighteen months he showed the essential passivity of his sexual aims, interrupting his parents' intercourse by passing a stool, thus expressing his sympathetic sexual excitement. His passivity transformed his sadism to its passive counterpart, masochism, though sadism persisted in his habit of tormenting small animals.

The reconstruction of the primal scene is only one strand in this complex case history, but from it we can see how psychoanalytic interpretation must employ not merely imaginative hypotheses, but the mental acrobatics and comic distortions of fantasy. Specific interpretations are derived from the meta-psychological theories, which are themselves derived from clinical cases. Patterns are elaborately constructed and then split up again so that elements in the story can be referred back, for example, to the theories of genital organisation and the defence functions of anxiety-hysteria. Identifications are made on the basis of theory (femininity = castration = passivity), and explanations are proffered for the substituted terms. The necessity of fantasy is not special to this case-history, in which the primal scene must admittedly be hypothesised, but to all good analysis, which appreciates the strangeness, the unexpected implications and unwieldly ramifications of its material, as well as the pitfalls inherent to the mind studying itself. In any such study terms and patterns must be created, and the creator borrows from known, agreed terms, patterns and structures, thus employing a language something like metaphor in that it proceeds by analogy, but different from it in that it is as primary a language as can here be used.

Freud, like any fantasist, persuades us that the usual is extraordinary and that commonplace explanations are inadequate. He levers open cracks in knowledge which he then fills with his stories, working repeatedly under the pressure of new ignorances discovered within the world he himself has created but which can also be seen to be our world. His *métier* was the labyrinth, for something 'new can be only gained from analyses that present special difficulties ... Only in such cases do we succeed in descending into the deepest and most primitive strata of mental development and in gaining from there solutions for the problems of later formulations.' Thus, like all great fantasists, he fought his way out of the maze his own imagination craved, and believed that there might eventually be a story to end all his stories: 'a single case does not give us all the information that we should like to have. Or, to put it more correctly, it might teach us everything, if we were not compelled by the inexperience of our own perception to content ourselves with a little.'[19] Though he insists that tact is an essential psychoanalytic procedure, arising from the possibility of error and the impossibility of discovering the entire truth,[20] he misconstrues the tentative nature of his aims themselves. In Freud's view, uncertainty and partiality result from the failure of his aims rather than from the nature of his quest. If, however, psychoanalysis is, as I suggest, more similar to a rich and complex fantasy work than to a set of explanatory theories, the uncertainty and partiality result, first, from the susceptibility of any text to amendment or restriction, and secondly, from the aims of the fantasist which are to differentiate peculiarly elusive phenomena, to reveal failure in understanding, to test and tease the borders of knowledge, to follow sensibility across those borders and record its anxious path, and (with the help of the critic) to show what we can bring back to normal life from that grey area in which knowledge and ignorance so outrageously couple. Certainty, predictability, irreducibility are not difficult quarries but impossible ones. Each representation is an experiment, an attempt to realise telling patterns and images, whatever their 'unreality'. Thus justice must be done to the role fantasy plays in such dubious and unstable, but enlightening and exciting investigations.

Notes

CHAPTER 1: Introduction: Fantasy and Psychoanalysis.

1. W. Shakespeare, *Romeo and Juliet,* Act 1, sc. iv, ll. 102-6.
2. Cf. Shoshana Felman, 'To Open the Question', *Yale French Studies,* 55-6 (1977).
3. All references to Sigmund Freud are from *The Standard Edition of the Complete Psychological Works,* henceforth *S.E.* (London: Hogarth Press, 1953-74), vol. 18, p. 17.
4. Cf. Harold Bloom, 'Freud's Concepts of Defense and the Poetic Will' and Humphrey Morris, 'The Need to Connect: Representations of Freud's Psychical Apparatus', in Joseph H. Smith (ed.), *The Literary Freud* (New Haven: Yale University Press, 1980). Also, Jean-Michel Rey, *Parcours de Freud* (Paris: Galilee 1974).
5. Cf. Kenneth Burke, 'Freud and the Analysis of Poetry', in *The Philosophy of Literary Form,* revised ed. (New York: University of California Press 1957); William Empson, *Seven Types of Ambiguity,* 3rd ed. (London: Chatto and Windus, 1970); and Graham Hough. A *Preface to 'The Faerie Queene'* (London: Longmans, 1962).
6. *S.E.,* Vol. 2, p. 160.
7. *S.E.,* Vol. 18, pp. 26-7.
8. *S.E.,* Vol. 22, p. 73.
9. *S.E.,* Vol. 23, p. 159.
10. *S.E.,* vol. 14, pp. 166-7.
11. For a somewhat distended discussion of the way in which material can be unconscious because it is formless rather than undesirable, see Anton Ehrenzweig, *The Hidden Order of Art* (London: Weidenfeld & Nicolson, 1967).

CHAPTER 2: Fantasy as Morality: Conrad's 'Heart of Darkness' and Hawthorne's *The Scarlet Letter.*

1. F.R. Leavis, *The Great Tradition* (Harmondsworth: Peregrine, 1962), pp. 198-9.
2. Joseph Conrad, 'Heart of Darkness' (New York: Bantam, 1971), pp. 128-31.
3. *Ibid.,* p. 112.
4. *Ibid.,* p. 98.
5. *Ibid.,* p. 25.
6. *Ibid.,* p. 119.

7. *Ibid.*, p. 44.
8. *Ibid.*, pp. 26-8.
9. *Ibid.*, p. 75.
10. *Ibid.*, p. 59.
11. *Ibid.*, p. 65.
12. Nathaniel Hawthorne, *The Scarlet Letter* (New York: New American Library, 1959), pp. 44-5.
13. *Three Tales from Conrad,* Douglas Brown (ed.), (London: Hutchinson, 1960), p. 77.
14. *The Scarlet Letter,* pp. 63-4.
15. *Ibid.*, p. 70.
16. *Ibid.*, p. 79.
17. *Ibid.*, pp. 122, 128.
18. *Ibid.*, p. 67.
19. E.g., D.H. Lawrence, *Studies in Classic American Literature* (Harmondsworth: Penguin, 1971).
20. *The Scarlet Letter,* p. 83.
21. *Ibid.*, p. 154.
22. *Ibid.*, pp. 79-80.
23. *Ibid.*, p. 73.
24. *Ibid.*, p. 139.
25. *Ibid.*, p. 147.
26. *Ibid.*, p. 205.
27. *Ibid.*, p. 127.
28. *Ibid.*, p. 242.

CHAPTER 3: The Uncanny: Freud, E.T.A. Hoffmann, Edgar Allan Poe.
1. *S.E.*, vol. 17, p. 219.
2. *S.E.*, vol. 17, p. 219.
3. Freud's essays on Dostoevsky and Leonardo are examples of this approach, and those who have followed in his footsteps have fared even worse, e.g., K.R. Eissler, *Leonardo da Vinci: Psychoanalytic Notes on the Enigma* (London: Hogarth Press, 1962), and Humberto Nagera, *Vincent Van Gogh* (London: Allen & Unwin, 1967).
4. *S.E.*, vol. 17, p. 232.
5. *The Best Tales of Hoffmann,* E.F. Bleiler (ed.), (New York: Dover, 1967), p. 193.
6. *Beyond the Pleasure Principle,* chapt. 2, *S.E.*, vol. 18.
7. Marie Bonaparte, *The Life and Works of Edgar Allan Poe, A Psycho-Analytic Interpretation* (John Rodker, trans.), (London: Imago, 1949).
8. *Ibid.*, p. 218.
9. *Ibid.*, pp. 240, 249.
10. *Ibid.*, p. 501.
11. *Ibid.*, pp. 465-9.

CHAPTER 4: The Double: Stevenson's *Dr Jekyll and Mr Hyde*, Hoffmann's *The Devil's Elixirs*, Dostoevsky's *The Double*.

1. *New Introductory Lectures* (1933), lecture 31, *S.E.*, vol. 22.
2. *S.E.*, vol. 18, pp. 105-10.
3. 'Leonardo da Vinci and a Memory of his Childhood', *S.E.*, vol. 11, p. 59.
4. 'Mourning and Melancholia' (1917), *S.E.*, vol. 14, p. 239.
5. Otto Rank, *Der Doppelgänger* (London: Imago, 1914).
6. *S.E.*, vol. 17, p. 235.
7. *S.E.*, vol. 17, p. 236.
8. *S.E.*, vol. 17, pp. 236-7.
9. *S.E.*, vol. 17, p. 233.
10. *S.E.*, vol. 14, p. 239.
11. E.T.A. Hoffmann, *The Devil's Elixirs*, Ronald Taylor (trans.), (London: Calder, 1963), pp. 226-8.
12. F. Dostoevsky, *The Double* Jessie Coulson (trans.), (Harmondsworth: Penguin, 1975), pp. 127-8.
13. *Ibid.*, p. 132.
14. *Ibid.*, p. 134.
15. *Ibid.*, p. 223.
16. *Ibid.*, p. 209.
17. Cf. *S.E.*, vol. 11, pp. 169-70.
18. *The Double*, pp. 167-171.
19. *Ibid.*, p. 237.

CHAPTER 5: Fantastic Objectivity: Franz Kafka.

1. Franz Kafka, *Wedding Preparations in the Country and other stories*, Willa and Edwin Muir (trans.), (Harmondsworth: Penguin, 1978), p. 129.
2. *Ibid.*, p. 114.
3. *Ibid.*, pp. 115-17.
4. J. Lacan, *Les Quatre Concepts foundamentaux de la psychanalyse* (Paris: Seuil, 1973), p. 158; I.A. Richards, *The Philosophy of Rhetoric* (New York: Oxford University Press, 1936). See also Shoshana Felman, 'Turning the Screw of Interpretation', *Yale French Studies*, 55-6 (1977), p. 133.
5. Anton Chekhov, *Lady with a Lapdog and other stories*, David Magarshack (trans.), (Harmondsworth: Penguin, 1977), pp. 137-8.
6. *The Interpretation of Dreams* (1900-01), *S.E.*, vol. 4, p. 260.
7. Nathaniel Hawthorne, 'Wakefield', in Newton Arvin (ed.), *Hawthorne's Short Stories* (New York: Vintage, 1946), p. 36.
8. Nikolai Gogol, *Dairy of a Madman and other stories*, Ronald Wilks (trans.), (Harmondsworth: Penguin, 1978), pp. 186-7. Reprinted by permission of Penguin Books Ltd.

9. *Ibid.*, pp. 23-4.

10. *Ibid.*, p. 20.

11. *Ibid.*, pp. 20. 24.

12. Kafka, *op. cit.*, p. 119.

13. *Ibid.*, p. 124.

14. Delmore Schwartz, *In Dreams Begin Responsibilities and other stories* (London: Secker & Warburg, 1978), p. 129.

15. *Ibid.*, p. 131.

16. *Ibid.*, p. 135.

17. *Ibid.*, p. 138.

18. *Ibid.*, p. 139.

19. Kafka, *op. cit.*, p. 106.

20. F. Dürrenmatt, *Grieche Sucht Griechin*, R. and C. Winston (trans.), (London: Cape, 1966).

CHAPTER 6: The Fantasy of Order: Vladimir Nabokov.

1. *Nabokov's Quartet* (London: Panther, 1972), p. 13.

2. *Ibid.*, p. 19.

3. *Ibid.*, p. 15.

4. *Ibid.*, p. 31.

5. *Ibid.*, pp. 23, 31.

6. *Ibid.*, p. 39.

7. *S.E.*, vol. 4, p. 245.

8. *Nabokov's Quartet*, p. 30.

9. *Ibid.*, pp. 33-4.

10. *Ibid.*, p. 124.

11. V. Nabokov, *The Defence*, Michael Scammell, in collaboration with the author (trans.), (London: Panther, 1973), pp. 73-4.

12. *Ibid.*, p. 78.

13. *Ibid.*, p. 16.

14. *Ibid.*, p. 105.

15. *Ibid.*, p. 81.

16. *Ibid.*, p. 109.

17. *Ibid.*, p. 173.

18. *Ibid.*, p. 198.

19. *Ibid.*, pp. 185-6.

20. V. Nabokov, *The Eye* (London: Weidenfeld & Nicolson, 1966), p. 103.

21. *Nabokov's Quartet*, p. 55.

22. *Ibid.*, p. 58.

23. *Ibid.*, p. 62.

24. *Ibid.*, p. 65.

25. *Ibid.,* pp. 76-8.

CHAPTER 7: Logical Fantasy: Jorge Luis Borges.
1. *Fictions,* E. Editores (trans.), (London: Calder, 1965), p. 24.
2. *Ibid.,* p. 33.
3. *Labyrinths,* Donald Yate and James Irby (eds.), (Harmondsworth: Penguin, 1972), p. 177. Originally in *The Aleph.*
4. *Ibid.,* p. 179.
5. From *Other Inquisitions* (Austin: University of Texas Press, 1964).
6. From *The Aleph.*
7. *Labyrinths,* p. 205.
8. From *Fictions.*
9. From *Fictions.*
10. *Fictions,* p. 63.
11. From *Fictions.*
12. *Fictions,* p. 72.
13. *Ibid.,* p. 76.
14. E.g. John Sturrock, *Paper Tigers* (London: Oxford University Press, 1977).
15. From *The Aleph.*
16. *Labyrinths,* p. 164.
17. *Ibid.,* p. 164.
18. *Ibid.,* p. 169.
19. From *The Aleph.*
20. *Labyrinths,* pp. 198-9.
21. *Ibid.,* p. 198.
22. *Ibid.,* pp. 201-2.
23. *Fictions,* p. 130.
24. *Ibid.,* pp. 131-2.
25. *Ibid.,* p. 153.
26. *Ibid.,* p. 154.
27. *Ibid.,* p. 154.
28. *Ibid.,* p. 155.
29. *Ibid.,* pp. 54-6.
30. *Ibid.,* pp. 57-8.
31. *Labyrinths,* p. 285.

CHAPTER 8: Psychoanalysis as Fantasy.
1. *Introductory Lectures,* lecture 5, *S.E.,* vol. 15, p. 83.
2. 'The Unconscious' (1915), *S.E.,* vol. 14, p. 161.
3. Cf., Kenneth Burke, *op. cit.,* William Empson, *op. cit.,* Graham Hough, *op. cit.*
4. For a discussion of techniques similar to dream and allegory interpretations see

Meredith Anne Skura, 'Revisions and Rereadings in Dreams and Allegories', in Joseph H. Smith, *The Literary Freud* (New Haven: Yale University Press, 1980). I am indebted to Skura's suggestive paper for many of the following points.

5. *S.E.,* vol. 5, p. 341.

6. Lionel Trilling, 'Freud: Within and Beyond Culture', in *Beyond Culture* (London: Secker & Warburg, 1966), p. 92.

7. *S.E.,* vol. 5, p. 566.

8. *S.E.,* vol. 12, p. 224.

9. Cf. 'Creative Writers and Day-Dreaming', *S.E.,* vol. 9, p. 143.

10. A.E. Jones, 'The Theory of Symbolism', in *Papers on Psychoanalysis,* 5th ed. (London: H. Karnac, 1948).

11. Melanie Klein, 'Symbol Formation and its Importance in the Development of the Ego', *International Journal of Psycho-Analysis,* vol. 11 (1930).

12. D.W. Winnicott, *Playing and Reality* (London: Tavistock Press, 1971).

13. Carl Jung, 'The Psychology of the Child Archetype', in *Collected Works,* vol. 9, (London: Routledge & Kegan Paul, 1959), p. 156.

14. *S.E.,* vol. 14, p. 149.

15. 'From the History of an Infantile Neurosis' *(1918), S.E.,* vol. 17, p. 3.

16. *S.E.,* vol. 17, p. 104.

17. For an example of the way in which subsequent analysis and subsequent theories supplement or modify Freud's discussion of this case, see Ruth Mack Brunswick, 'A Supplement to Freud's "History of an Infantile Neurosis" ', in Muriel Gardiner (ed.), *The Wolf-Man* (New York: Basic Books, 1971).
For a discussion of the way in which the new analysis might bring to light new childhood material, see J. Hárnik, 'Kritisches über Mack Brunswicks Nachtrag zu Freuds "Geschichte einer infantilen Neurose" ', *Internationale Zeitschrift für Psychoanalyse,* (1930), vol. 16, pp. 123-7; Ruth Mack Brunswick, 'Entgegnung auf Hárniks Kritische Bemerkungen, *Internationale Zeitschrift für Psychoanalyse,* (1930) vol. 16, pp. 128-9; J. Hárnik, Erwiderung auf Mack Brunswicks Entgegnung', *Internationale Zeitschrift für Psychoanalyse,* (1931), vol. 17, pp. 400-2; Ruth Mack Brunswick, 'Schlusswort', *Internationale Zeitschrift für Psychoanalyse,* (1931), vol. 17, p. 402.

18. *S.E.,* vol. 17, p. 29.

19. *S.E.,* vol. 17, p. 10.

20. *S.E.,* vol. 11, p. 226.

INDEX